NINJA FIGHTING TECHNIQUES

NINJA FIGHTING TECHNIQUES

A MODERN APPROACH TO SELF-DEFENSE AND AVOIDING CONFLICT

STEPHEN K. HAYES

TUTTLE Publishing

Tokyo | Rutland, Vermont | Singapore

Please note that the publisher and author of this instructional book are NOT RESPONSIBLE in any manner whatsoever for any injury that may result from practicing the techniques and/or following the instructions given within. Martial arts training can be dangerous—both to you and to others—if not practiced safely. If you're in doubt as to how to proceed or whether your practice is safe, consult with a trained martial arts teacher before beginning. Since the physical activities described herein may be too strenuous in nature for some readers, it is also essential that a physician be consulted prior to training.

CONTENTS

DEDICATION

This book is dedicated to my dear friend Tenzin Gyatso, 14th Dalai Lama of Tibet. Throughout our years together, you showed me the other half of cultivating warrior protector strength, vision, and dignity.

ACKNOWLEDGEMENTS

I started in my teens studying martial arts which, in 1960s America, was a strange and little-understood activity. Eight years later, in the 1970s, I journeyed to Japan in a hunt for the then elusive ninja, determined to learn their martial arts. In the 1980s, I brought the unheard of martial art of the ninja back to America, and taught willing people the intricacies through seminars and my smash hit books. In the 1990s, I felt the need to upgrade the 1500s mechanics of the ninja martial art to better fit the physical realities and the psychological demands of 21st century America, giving birth to the legacy of To-Shin Do.

This, then, is my first acknowledgement for this book: I express my deepest appreciation for all those fellow students who trained alongside of me and encouraged me along my more than 50 years of martial arts. You granted me the ability to pursue my heart's longing for the utmost in warrior protector skill training day in and day out. I was blessed to never ever have "a real job." Throughout the decades I was free to pursue full-time the evasive knowledge, thanks to your support of me through buying books, subscribing to our internet service, and enrolling in my seminars and my personal school. I am truly honored in this lifetime, and I know it.

I also must secondly acknowledge the loving care of my family who allowed me to devote my days to martial and meditative study—from parents, Ira and Carol, who supported me as I awakened to my life's calling, to my wife Rumiko who shared the joyful and yet terrifying years of developing To-Shin Do, to my daughters Reina and Marissa who grew up in the dojo with their parents, and now to my grandkids who wave swords and tumble around the dojo with me.

Thirdly, I appreciate and acknowledge all my fellow warriors who agreed to be the action models in this latest volume of modern ninja personal protection. Just one more example of folks gathering together to celebrate my vision as their commitment to their own growth. Beautiful. Thank you so much.

My salute? To all who encouraged me to be exactly what I was born to be.

An-shu Stephen and An-shu Rumiko Hayes at the beginning of the legacy that became To-Shin Do.

INTRODUCTION
How This Book Came to Be

On a sunny afternoon in the fall of 1963, a friend and I were walking home from middle school. We passed the drug store, where at the soda fountain counter sat the notorious Philip "Sonny" Mantia along with his buddies. He was three years older than the rest of us in our class, as he had spent three years in juvenile prison. Mantia had 26 felonies to his name, most of which were aggressive fights he had been convicted of starting and finishing.

To my shock, Mantia and his buddies suddenly poured out of the drug store and surrounded us. In confusion I tried to reason with the aggressors, but they focused their attention on my friend. Had he done something to rouse their wrath? It was all happening so fast. My mind spun in bewilderment. I was not ready at all.

Mantia was shouting at my friend, taunting him with abrupt shoves. Horrified, I stood and stared. I was frozen, unable to move. Some of Mantia's cohorts surrounded my friend so that he could not escape. Two of them positioned themselves in front of me so that I could not move to my friend's aid.

I was 13 then. Up to that point, I had experienced only a few playground skirmishes with bullies at school. Most of those encounters had been mere shoving and shouting and amateurish grappling, and were over with before anyone had been seriously hurt.

This guy was another reality altogether. He had grabbed my friend by the wrist and was spinning him around in a circle, increasing his speed and jerking until my friend was on his knees in the dust. Once he had him down, Mantia began pounding his fists into the back of my friend's head. He was swearing horrifically, using savage language shocking to my young ears in the 1960s.

An older man walked by and saw what was happening, and shouted at Mantia and his buddies to knock it off. But the hangers-on moved at him aggressively and chased him away with curses and threatening fists. Time moved in agonizing slow motion. I beheld in horror Mantia's fists bouncing off the back of my friend's head. Swearing fiercely and swinging his arms in over and over, he appeared to be the embodiment of pure uncontrolled raging evil.

I felt cold. I was doubtless shaking. Cut off by the older boys blocking my way, I was powerless to help my friend. But truth told, those boys blocking me had little threat from me. I was immobilized, paralyzed with shock and trepidation and adrenalized lock-up. I stood there frozen. My mouth twisted in a silent scream. I was incapable of moving. I watched in horror as my friend went from resisting, to attempting to cover from the blows, to defeated resignation. I could not believe what was happening.

And then it was all over. Mantia was done. He and his buddies moved as a pack of wolves back to the drug store, tossing savage insults at us over their shoulders. My friend rose to his feet. Amazingly, he was still very conscious, and no blood was showing from the pummeling he had taken. He dusted himself off, mumbled something, and we were once again walking home.

I was so furious and confused and embarrassed. I could not speak. We walked in silence, awkwardly trying to put the past moments behind us. But deep inside, something primordial had come awake in me. A strange blend of rage, and oddly at the same time compassion, overwhelmed me.

I vowed I would do whatever it took to never be forced to stand by in helplessness while a pure and wholesome innocent took a beating again. I had no idea how I would do it. But I would make a difference in the world. I would find a way to stand up to senseless violence, to stop it in its tracks. When others chose brutality and savagery, I would make there be peace. I would be there for the defenseless. I would show the beautiful and kind the way to temporarily become a raging force for good.

I knew of no martial arts schools in Dayton, Ohio, back then. I had no idea how I would accomplish my vows. I only knew in my core that I would devote my life to righting the wrong I had just witnessed. I made a solemn promise. I pledged a holy vow.

Thus Began a Life of Studying Violence and How to Overcome It

In 1967 I picked Miami University in Oxford, Ohio, because I had seen a boy in a white *do-gi* training suit walking in the gym. "Must be a member of the judo club," commented the tour guide casually when I quickly grabbed him and asked about the boy. I made up my mind right then and there that I would attend Miami. At last I would begin my long-awaited study of judo, the Japanese secrets of self-defense called "the supple art."

Unfortunately, once I got to campus, it turned out there was no judo club at Miami. The guide had been mistaken. There was however a Tang Soo Do training group. But it was run by a Navy Commander and restricted to members of the Navy ROTC in the Vietnam War days. Daunted but nonetheless determined, I somehow prevailed on the Commander to accept me, even though I was not in the Navy. I took to Tang Soo Do training with an unexcelled passion. Nobody at Miami trained harder. Nobody was more determined. None made practice sessions more often than I did.

Years of training added up. During summers away from college, I trained with other martial arts clubs wherever I went. I made Black Belt by late in my junior year.

One evening during a play rehearsal in my senior year, when a group of us was sitting around waiting to go on, I got to chatting with a fellow theater student. He had grown up a tough street scrapper in a miserably poor neighborhood, but had miraculously ended up at the university. I was telling him about my karate training, a strange and rare thing back in those days. I demonstrated a twisting punch to his up-held palm. The punch started out up-side-down, pierced straight out, and twisted into palm-down position at the moment of impact. I held my shoulder upright and in place. His hand moved back with the hit.

The boy cocked his head in admiration. "Wow! I've never seen anything like that. So cool!" He then looked aside, seemingly in embarrassment. "On the streets, we'd just throw our fists and hide behind them until we connected." He lifted his hand and leaned in with his shoulder and sent a loose relaxed looping strike that suddenly tightened into a hit against my up-held palm. The smack noise and follow-through sent my hand flying back behind my shoulder.

I was stunned. In all of my years of Tang Soo Do training, I had never dealt with a typical American street punch. If someone had thrown one of those at me in anger, I had no idea how I would have responded. It was a chilling revelation of my ignorant vulnerability.

My world collapsed. I felt breathless, naked, and invaded. I was confused and angry. How could my training completely ignore the reality of the streets like that? At the same time, I felt strangely excited. Instantly I was somehow bigger and freer than I had been. It was indeed a huge world out there — the study of violence and how to subdue it — and I was in an instant more awake than I had ever been. I would take that freedom and rejoice in it. I would follow it as far as I could for as long as it took.

Now Fifty Years Later...

Throughout the decades of my involvement in the Asian martial and meditation disciplines, my own purpose continued to be to discover those methods, attitudes, and insights that could advance me in my quest. I ran out of lessons in karate and boxing, and I became disappointed in champions my own age who had succumbed to the allure of ego, who lived shattered lives, and were victims of the drug culture of the 1970s. I turned my attention to Japan and the long-admired secret art of the ninja. I had read

Meditation plays an important role in gaining control of the mind's reactions in To-Shin Do.

about the mysterious art in a James Bond novel in high school. I would go to Japan. I would meet and train with elders who handed down the ninja martial art for generations of secrecy. I would learn punching and kicking skills of course. But I would also learn the grappling and choking and weapons that I had so missed in my training. Also hinted at were the secrets of mental and even spiritual power that awaited.

Ninja training in Japan turned out to be quite different from what I had expected. The dojo was tiny, a mere cleared out storage room in the grandmaster's house. In remote Noda City, student numbers were extremely small—15 at the highest. 33rd Togakure Ryu ninja grandmaster Toshitsugu Takamatsu had just died over a year before, and the 34th grandmaster Masaaki Hatsumi was using those few nights per week to review and explore what he had been taught.

There was no curriculum at all. There was no class for beginners as opposed to senior practitioners. All just trained together in the tiny room. Random *kata* fight examples were read from handwritten books and acted out. Most times, the kata was not identified as to its *ryu* lineage or scroll.

Things would start out far apart. A punch or kick or grab would bring the training partners closer to each other. A defense or two would be thrown up. Control of the attacker would be gained. He would be taken to the ground where he was broken or killed. Each student kept his own notes as to what was studied each night.

1980s outdoor seminars gave the author a chance to test his martial arts.

After only a short time, it became clear to me that this was not a training hall where clear and paced instruction was the usual approach. More often than not, I had to "steal" the technique being practiced. The seniors would try out various movements without explanation. Techniques would be performed differently from man to man. I had to pay close attention to discrimination. I had to find my own way in the middle of all the variations I saw. I had to find my own movements.

Techniques were presented in literal form from the many books handed down from Takamatsu Sensei. I began to sense that not all things practiced in the dojo were fully understood by the practitioners. Years became decades. I came to focus on bridging the gap between source and destination realities. What was the hidden meaning behind why that technique was preserved? What was the abstract principle being transmitted in the concrete movements of the *kata*? What was the key?

I discovered I had a knack for diving into an ancient foreign culture and extracting principles that I would translate to fit my own culture back home. That involved knowing very well the foreign culture as well as my own. I went to the East and brought back unheard of information to the West. I traversed the time span from ancient hidden conceptions to modern broad-based applications.

While I shared what I discovered with all who would listen, it has been an admittedly intimately personal career. I have sought out experiences and contacts with the purpose of positively advancing my own physical, intellectual, and spiritual being. I still explore to a significant degree every day. I am a product of all I have faced. I continue to refine.

Because of my intensely transformative involvement in my subject matter, it has been impossible to even pretend to be capable of a classical scholar's aloofness from that which he studies. I *am* that which I study. I have always internalized all experiences gathered in the pursuit of knowledge. Some of those experiences were taken to heart and formed internally held concepts. Other experiences were rejected as not relevant to my needs. Nonetheless, all knowledge encountered was happily (and sometimes not so happily) experienced from the inside looking out.

I became well known for my pioneering work as the first American to become a dedicated disciple of the 34 generation old Togakure Ryu ninja tradition in Japan. What I encountered in 1975 when I first entered the Japanese dojo seemed revolutionary. So many mind-expanding ideas were a dizzying delight. I described my eye-opening adventures with the ninja in my very first book, *The Ninja and Their Secret Fighting Art*, published in 1981 and now available in a newly revised edition from Tuttle.

As the years went by, it became increasingly obvious that the Japanese teachers were practicing an antiquated fighting art. They seemed loyally dedicated to preserving Eastern ways of the past. They were not particularly interested in exploring modern Western ways of attacking and handling aggressors.

Unconventional techniques are standard fare in To-Shin Do.

In the mid 1990s, 20 years after I had entered the ninja dojo, I was compelled to create a modern Western art based on timeless ninja principles aimed at solving contemporary challenges. We needed an updated method of ninja protector combat for today. I described the basics of my modern self-defense program in *The Ninja Defense*, published by Tuttle in 2012.

It would be awkward to use an established historical name like *ninjutsu* to describe my contemporary personal protection system. I needed a term to differentiate between the classical ninja martial arts I had been taught and the modern form I built. To label my modern version of ancient *ninjutsu*, I came up with the new name To-Shin Do. The new name is based on the form of the old name. I separated the single letter character for *nin* 忍 of *ninja* and their secret art of *ninjutsu* into two parts (minus a small dash). *To* 刀 for "sword" carries the meaning of our technology—how we practice survival fighting. *Shin* 心 for "heart" communicates our intention—how we evaluate the moment to moment decisions as to what to do and when. Do 道 translates as "road" for the pathway to mastery—a lifetime of exploration if necessary.

An-shu Rumiko gives pointers at a training convention.

This is not something I just made up or pulled together. From roots deep in the principles of classic Japanese ninja martial arts, To-Shin

Do training is a thorough system of personal preparation for facing the kinds of conflict and opposition that can surprise us in the course of daily living. Our training program leads to the ability to live life fully, fearlessly, and freely.

The lessons in our training method are based on ancient well-tested warrior disciplines handed down through historical martial traditions I studied with the ninja grandmaster in Japan. I also include the spiritual and ethical lessons I learned traveling with Tenzin Gyatso, the Dalai Lama of Tibet, as his personal security escort in the 1990s. At the same time, To-Shin Do training is built around a very modern approach to handling successfully the kind of threats and confrontations most likely in our own contemporary culture, and for seeking answers to the deepest questions of life. In what ways do your martial discoveries parallel the conflicts you face in the workplace, at home, in school, or out in the marketplace?

When I put this book together, I was admittedly conflicted as to what I intended to include. The ego part of me wanted to include outrageous advanced material, things that would impress seasoned martial artists. But this book is not designed for martial artists with oh-so-many years of training. It is to be used along with *The Ninja Defense*. This book specifically targets intermediate students looking to learn valuable survival techniques and advance their skills and knowledge about dangerous confrontation. The attacks come more from YouTube clips than UFC footage or the ancient scrolls of Japan. "What would a street hostile throw at us," was more the consideration than what professional competitors or warriors of another age might do. What about those assaults that surprise us, catch us off-guard, cause us to take a moment of doubt to recognize what is happening? That is what I wanted to address in this book.

To-Shin Do was developed from an ancient Japanese ninja model. Intelligence agents needed a fighting system to cover their escape from a compromised mission. The assumption was that fighting is way down on the list of possible ways of restoring peace. How do you handle a potentially murderous situation with unknown numbers of assailants? This is very different from a fighting system designed to go as many rounds as needed to defeat another person who has agreed to a contest of skills.

To-Shin Do is a realistic martial arts training system that includes instruction in techniques and strategies for dealing with:

- grappling, throwing, choking, and joint-locking
- striking, kicking, and punching

- stick, blade, cord, and projectile weapons
- handling multiple assailants and surprise attacks
- overcoming psychological intimidation or bullying

The hanbo *cane is one of the traditional ninja weapons.*

Through exposure to the physical, intellectual, and spiritual challenges posed in the many facets of our training program, you will gain first-hand experience in identifying and enhancing those aspects of your life that facilitate growth, confidence, peace of mind, and the joy that accompanies living well and powerfully. You will change and grow and advance as a human being. You will be bigger, broader, with more resources to draw from.

To-Shin Do martial arts training is as well founded on a very strong and bluntly stated code of mindful action — how to live a worthy noble life. You cannot learn how to become a winner by spending time with losers. Ally yourself with proven role models who have been through the battles and can demonstrate what powerful living looks like. You will develop the momentum of accomplishment that leads to being a winner in life. It is that simple.

I am still inspired to this day by exaggerated images of intelligence, compassion, and strength I saw in TV shows, novels, and movies of my youth. You mean there is a tradition of inspiration for people longing for mythic-level self-expansion, in pursuit of an ideal so high that we never will surpass it? I have to have that!

Author An-shu Stephen K. Hayes with some of the leaders of To-Shin Do today.

Preparation for the cultivation of new strengths begins with intelligence gathering. Enjoy this book, and any new awareness it might spark in your life. Discuss its ideas with others. Remember to re-read these chapters several times. Look for the direct applications to life right now. Use the insights to plan ahead for future confidence and power. By all means, use it to inspire ever more happiness in your life. The world needs your bright strength. We are counting on you.

Graduates at author's home dojo in Ohio.

PART 1

First Considerations

CHAPTER 1
Sensing Potential Danger

Modern martial arts have increasingly been "sportified" in the years following World War II and the introduction of the Asian martial traditions to America and Europe. This trend is very important to explore. It is crucial to examine the results of what this has brought to Westerners. It may be quite different from what the Asian martial arts may have originally intended to cultivate.

In a sports contest, the player takes defined objectives and methods and applies them under pressure. His goal is to win over rival competitors in producing the specific results that define victory. Therefore, in a martial sport, the specific methods and definition of victory are very important. It is also true that rules generally prevent the loser from dying.

An-shu Rumiko gives pointers at a training convention.

Successful self-protection is a very different process. Factors such as culture, laws, morality, and self-determined social roles weigh heavily in the moment to moment decision making process. Victory or defeat is often self-determined. We decide what is success and failure. Techniques are valued solely on their ability to produce results that lead to that self-defined victory.

Everyone understands that I am in no way disparaging competitors, of course. I enjoy watching great championship wins. I am just stating that such things are very different from my ultimate purposes in martial training. My commitment to students is that To-Shin Do will remain the most honest and useful method of preparing for successful self-protection possible. The nature of that promise requires us to continue to grow as a technology for learning how to produce better results. The nature of that promise in turn is that techniques for achieving the goal will continue to evolve.

Stephen and Rumiko Hayes travel the world as seminar presenters, sharing To-Shin Do secrets.

It is also true that the methods used by aggressors to dominate others change and mutate over time and social conditions as well. Therefore, a truly useful self-protection training method will have to grow and evolve in order to keep up with the development of new forms of aggression, domination, and assault. It is my strong belief that a martial art that does not address directly the specifics of the aggressor's approach cannot be thought of as an effective method for producing real-world results. This is admittedly my strong belief. Obviously there are others who disagree with my premise, though their arguments often sound more like defensive-rationalization instead of reason.

Here's a comparison to help understand. Think of contrasting the study of self-protection martial arts with going to law school. Would you really want to study with a classical teacher if real-world practical results were your goal? If you wanted to be the best possible attorney, how would you feel about enrolling under a teacher who boasted, "I am proud to say that I teach the exact same law that my teacher's teacher taught back in 1943... but you can kind of wiggle around in it and up-date it on your own if that's what you want."

In the dojo in Japan in the 1970s, there was heavy emphasis on what 16th Century aggressors would throw at a defender. These attacks were based on the ways people moved, the way they dressed, and the environmental conditions of those days. Every technique ended with the aggressor on the ground maimed to the point of total immobilization, and more often than not, dead or dying. It goes without saying that there were no legal systems to protect or prosecute in those days.

In the dojo in Japan in the 1970s, the classics were taught and practiced, just as they had been for generations of Japanese history. This was the ninja martial art, in all of its oddities. Many of the techniques were performed in strange ways designed to keep the aggressor from seeing the face of the defender. There were methods for escaping burning buildings with *tatami* rice mat floors and cedar plank ceilings, mainstays of Japanese architecture of the time. Many of the techniques involved unusual hidden weapons that would be impractical or illegal today. And if you do happen to be a counter-intelligence agent, modern technology far outshines the capabilities of crude 500-year-old iron, bamboo, and twine implements. We never covered anything like defending against boxer jabs, grappler submissions, kick boxer round kicks, and small group verbal-hassle surprise muggings. Those were not things that were threats in the Japan of the 1500s.

My teacher told me in 1982, when he was living in my house in Ohio on a trip from Japan, that he did not believe many people could fully grasp the ninja way of thinking and seeing. I disagreed with him strongly at the time. I even argued with him about it—politely, of course. Throughout the 1980s I tried to teach the ninjutsu I had learned in Japan

Ninja festival summer training camp in the 1980s.

in the 1970s. But by the early 1990s, I understood what he was trying to tell me. When I started my school in 1996, I set ninjutsu off to the side and offered a modern adaptation that was much more appropriate for the times.

Situational Awareness Is Not a Part of Sports Competition

Since To-Shin Do is a realistic approach to street and field violence, we have to take into consideration a lot more than sport martial artists do. In a competitive sport fighting ring, you know why the other guy is there. He and you have agreed to a contest of fighting skills. All you need to do is be a better, more athletic, or craftier fighter.

On the street, things get more complex. You may first have to decide whether a fight is going to happen. You have to evaluate whether this can simply be walked away from, or whether you need strong communication skills, or whether physical defensive skills must be used. You have to make a decision as to how many attackers there are. Then you have to go to work to end it as quickly as possible. Then you have to get out of there immediately.

This involves a whole world of evaluation skills not needed in a sport fight. You will require careful and timely reliance on situational awareness. And one key to effective situational awareness is observation. You will have to watch and consider situations, things, and people. Make ever-changing decisions based on what you see. Most of the time, simply seeing the potential that lies ahead can give you an advantage over people who drift through life blind to danger. But you will need ongoing training in developing and practicing such situational awareness.

Our internal triggers can unfortunately get us into what might be avoidable fights. An aggressor tries his best to guess what will trigger us into freezing up or flying out of control. We react to his button-pushing with emotional responses if he is in control of the situation. These internal triggers include anger, passion, fear, fear of being afraid, self-esteem, demand for respect, vulnerability to insults, road rage, turf challenges, or some honor code we live by. If you cannot control yourself internally, you will likely knee-jerk react externally, using your martial arts to engage in physical fighting. Might it be worth something in the long run to practice not losing your cool? Staying in charge? How many instructors teach such self control? How many have even considered such teaching? If you cannot control yourself, you will have a hard time controlling others.

Here are some ideas that might help in a typical street confrontation. On the street, these become important considerations. See how many you can identify with.

The Body informs. The way a person carries themselves gives us insight as to how they could become a threat. Body language shows subconscious and pre-conscious intentions through posture, facial expression, eye direction, hand positions, and movement. As a student practitioner of self protection skills, you come to realize that body language gives us advance warning—actions a person is about to take—and gives a glimpse into his mind—tells us his current thought state. Is he outwardly hostile? Is he trying to act noncommittal to get closer to us? Is he bluffing, testing us? Is he trying to conceal his true intentions? Is he huffing and puffing but with no real intention to fight?

The Face is the most expressive body part. It is also the most easily manipulated. Experienced attackers may control their facial expressions so as to be unreadable. The inexperienced might crack nervous grins, adopt frowns, dart their eyes, or display facial twitches. It is important to look past the signs that can be controlled and manipulated, and focus on those that cannot:

- Pupil dilation: The human fight or flight reaction is something few people can control. The brain signals the body to dump adrenaline into the bloodstream, raising the heart rate and making the pupils larger. As the pupils dilate, the peripheral vision narrows. It is a mechanism designed to bring us face to face with the threat directly. People about to act aggressively or perform a violent act will usually find their pupils dilated.

- Pulse: As aggressive impulse builds, the heart rate increases along with blood pressure. This can result in a pounding pulse visible in the neck and temples. This is difficult or impossible for most people to control.
- Sweat: An increased heart rate causes involuntary perspiration, which most aggressors cannot control well.
- Mouth: Besides obvious expressions, an open mouth often occurs when a person is breathing rapidly and can't get enough air from just their nose.
- Upper Torso: A person who is about to charge in will often telegraph his intention by the way he carries himself. The upper torso reveals two important tips. The first clue is the shoulders. Are the shoulders hanging naturally in a relaxed pose? Or are they tight and raised? The second clue is the upper chest area. What does his respiration tell you? Do you see a rapid chest rise and fall as evidence of breathing hard? When the action amps up, an aggressor tends to breathe shallowly from high in the chest.
- Hands and Arms: It's important to watch the hands closely at all times. Hands hovering around the waistband might represent a threat. At any moment, he could produce a weapon. Also, while balled fists are an obvious sign of aggression, keep in mind that many attacks come from the time-biding position of tightly crossed arms, or hands forcefully shoved into pockets.
- Legs and Feet: Is he moving, darting here and there nervously? Is he standing planted in place? Is he inching forward? Is he holding ground but leaning in with his upper body? We are looking for stance. Sometimes people blade themselves towards a perceived threat. Blading refers to a combat stance, where the dominant foot is behind the non-dominant foot and about shoulder width apart. Blading can also serve another purpose – most people carrying a concealed weapon will subconsciously pull the weapon side away from the threat, to protect it, conceal it, or cover a draw into action..

- The Whole Package: Look for movement warning signs, nervous twitches that signal that the person is about to act. Two common signs of impending action are pacing and standing on the balls of the feet. Many attacks begin with pacing back and forth and then launching an attack at the midpoint. Many flights or escapes begin with the person getting up on the balls of their feet, much as a runner would before the starting gun goes off.
- Violating your personal space by moving in and out of what is an apparent danger zone can be a way of intimidating you or testing you out. If you realize an aggressor is doing this to you, you can make a statement in a calm, slow, but firm voice, careful to not display any fear, unease, or anger. "I'm cool talking with you about this, but I need you to step back. You are way too close."

Humor and out of place familiarity work to let street scammers and muggers distract you. Watch for the too-friendly stranger, smiling big and talking on and on with cheerful questions thrown at you. Their goal is to get close enough for a knockout punch or incapacitating grab to start their assault. Often these guys are big and could damage you even without the subterfuge. But this way they get off without your defense or a risk to themselves. If you can touch the other person, they are too close. They can touch you too. Most street criminals will not give you warning signs. They will distract you and move in close to sucker punch you and follow up with punches, kicks, and throws.

Here are some things to consider:

Your name—If they overhear your name, they can use it to get closer. Hearing your name throws you off guard. You are distracted momentarily wondering how this person knows you. They gain a way to get that much closer to you.

Tricky tactics—Be wary of a person who is overly nice and talkative and tries to lure you in. Too much chatter with too many details and questions can be an attempt to get your guard down. Also watch out for the "man in trouble" and the stranger helping and trying to get you to help. Both men are scammers trying to trick you. Marauders in some airports have learned to target rental car drivers. They tap them with a rear bumper "accident." When the confused and out of place person gets out to see what happened, it turns into an attack. And of course a panhandler using a request for money is a classic ruse to get close enough to test you out and see if you are worthy of an attack.

Paying attention to your surroundings—Do not walk around with headphones on, ear buds in, or your eyes glued to a cellphone screen. This leaves you unaware and more of a target. So many are alarmingly ignorant with their head down and their life inside a bubble. They are easy prey. They feel secure in their own world and do not realize how attractive and easy they appear as a victim.

There are more than one—Especially near public transportation stations you might find teams working as a pack. These are often youths. They never attack one on one, but instead mount group assaults against singular victims. They communicate with a series of glances and head nods to reach consensus of whom the target should be and when to initiate the attack. Often one will act as the "mouth," confronting you or asking probing questions while the others surreptitiously position behind and beside you before an attack starts.

Assault Is Not Imminent, but Highly Possible...

If you end up confronted by a person who presents the following signs, your awareness and self protection strategies should go on alert. By all means, create distance. Body language should be grounded, confident, and assertive, but not threatening. And realistically, perhaps you might be ready to let the person vent verbally. You are the bigger, happier, more advanced person. You look down and have pity on them. Theirs is a troubled life, a life of lack. Maybe letting them spout off will be enough to satisfy them, as long as they use up energy (and not build up energy). Be sure they are not increasing in volume and rage. A fight might be avoided.

- Head, neck, and shoulders go back; person makes himself look bigger
- Face is dark red, splotchy, twitching as blood rushes up
- Lips are pushed forward bearing teeth; this may be a mirthless smile with wide open eyes
- Breathing is fast and shallow, preparing the body for fight, flight, or hyper-vigilance
- Beads of sweat appear on the face or neck
- Thousand-mile glare right through you; he avoids your gaze
- Exaggerated body and limb movements

The key to throws? Move into the attacker's center to unbalance him.

- "Eye rape" — a male slowly runs his gaze up and down a female defender's body
- Finger pointing and jerking head pecking
- Totally ignores you when you speak to him
- Gives you excessive attention during normal conversation; leans in with direct uninterrupted eye contact stare
- Goes from totally un-cooperative to totally cooperative, setting you up; normal people do not go from hot to cold - they need time to de-escalate
- Directs anger towards other inanimate items such as chairs or walls

- Moves in and out of your personal space, establishing dominance or testing your response

Assault Is Imminent. Here It Comes!

In the following group of signs, you likely have only a few seconds to react before your assailant attacks. If talking your way out will not work, might it be better to rely on a first strike approach? Continue with a compound attack until your aggressor is no longer a risk.

- Face goes from red to white, or ashen in dark skinned individuals; blood leaves the surface of the body and goes to the big muscles and organs needed for survival
- Lips tighten over teeth
- Breathing is fast and deep
- Change of stance, their body blades and shoulder drops
- Hands close into fists; you may see whites of knuckles with hands so tight
- Bobbing up and down or rocking back and forth on feet, the body's way to mask becoming adrenalized and hide the initial movement of a first strike
- Target glance; he looks where he is going to hit, or where he is going to escape after his attack
- Crouching and pulling head and chin down; body wants to protect the airway
- Eyebrows brought forward into a squinting frown; the body wants to protect the eyes
- Stops all movements and freezes in place
- Dropping center or lowering body like a cat or dog preparing to pounce
- Shedding clothes; takes off his hat, coat, or shirt prior to assault
- From full sentences to one-syllable replies as reptile brain takes over

The foregoing are just suggestions as to what to look for. Obviously, without a lot of experience dealing with dangerous people, you yourself may end up adrenalized with tunnel vision and hearing impairment and miss these or other cues. Continuous practice is absolutely required. The more you familiarize yourself with angry or deranged people, the more reliably you will be able to predict their future actions. This will leave you more in command over tense moments.

CHAPTER 2

Transforming Your Nature into Power

Think back to a time when you were suddenly forced into an argument, a battle of wits, or maybe even a physical fight. Can you recall in *specific terms* the texture of your feelings? How did you feel when faced with hostility? What was your initial reaction? What was brought about internally? What did you want to happen?

Whether your antagonist wants to argue with you, demoralize you, or beat you up, according to traditional ninja martial arts, one of *five potential response patterns* emerges from your inner core. These five possible reactions to hostility come from one of five inner centers. Your inner response would probably fit into one of the following five categories:

1. You immediately wanted things to *go back to the way they were* before they became an explosive and dangerous situation. You hold your ground. If your feelings could have spoken directly, your expression would have been something like, "Stop it! Stop it right now!"
2. You immediately wanted to *be in a better position,* where you could better control the explosive and dangerous situation. You tactically reposition for strategic advantage. If your feelings could have spoken directly, your expression would have been something like, "Oh no you don't! That's not going to work!"
3. You immediately wanted to *reach in and take control* of where the explosive and dangerous situation was going. You grab initiative in the unfolding process. If your feelings could have spoken directly, your expression would have been something like, "Hey! You want a fight? Really? *Really*?"
4. You immediately wanted to *escape to a place of invulnerability* from which you could cope with the explosive and dangerous situation. You

slip by, evade, escape the action, and disappear. If your feelings could have spoken directly, your expression would have been something like, "Easy! Easy. I'm not getting involved with this!"

5. You immediately produced some sort of *distracting or unexpected response* to throw off the explosiveness and danger of the situation. You restructure the entire dynamic of the threat. If your feelings could have spoken directly, perhaps your expression would have been something like, "I'm really above your needs, so let's see if we can find someone who would enjoy fighting with you."

Historically, basic ninja combat tactics are classified by a collection of five elements that symbolize these five responses. *Chi, sui, ka, fu, ku,* 地 水 火 風 空 or earth, water, fire, wind, and the void are the labels describing specific ninja *taijutsu* unarmed combat techniques.

Back in the 1970s when I asked the ninja grandmaster to explain the meaning of the five elements, he replied, "Don't worry about it. It's a part of old time Japanese religion. No need to bother with that."

"I'm not worried about it. I just want to know what it means." I said.

He shook his head in dismissal. "To understand that, you would need to go off to some mountaintop monastery and study with monks."

Years later, I realized he had not been giving me an order. He really was trying to tell me that it was not necessary to go to those extremes of understanding. But I had taken it as an order. I had indeed gone on to spend years studying with Japanese and Tibetan monks. And what I gained was a precious treasure, completely unrealized by many of my fellow Japanese students.

Knowledge of the significance of the five elements can be traced back to Indian Vedic lore, Tibetan Buddhist secret teachings, and then Japanese Shugendo mountain asceticism and Mikkyo esoteric Japanese Buddhist interpretations. The five element classification also found its way westward, and can be seen in Greek and European counterparts.

The *go-dai* 五 大 five elements are a code for the building blocks of the universe.

- *Chi* (earth) represents all things that are solid and firm. Bones, and rocks and mountains are examples. This is related to holding your ground in a fight.
- *Sui* (water) stands for all things that are fluid and flowing. Blood and rivers and oceans are examples. This is related to tactically reposi-

tioning for strategic advantage in a fight.

- *Ka* (fire) is all that generates warmth or growth. Metabolism, or flames or the sun are examples. This is related to preemptively closing in and intercepting in a fight.
- *Fu* (wind) represents movement or going from place to place. Breath, or wind or clouds are examples. This is related to moving freely to escape or evade in a fight.
- *Ku* (void) that unseen quality that supports all the other elements. The spaces in the body, or spaces between objects or outer space are examples. This is related to changing the dynamic of a fight, thereby confusing your attacker.

Earth (square), water (sphere), fire (triangle), wind ("bowl"), and void (teardrop, at top), show the five Japanese elementary progressions.

The reader should be aware that in some ninja schools today, unfortunately, the five elements have sadly been reduced to a mere counting system. They are used simply as a kind of shorthand for listing things, as we in the west would use "a, b, c, d" to create a list. There is no implicit meaning to the elemental terms taught. In such schools, the logic behind the five elements has long ago been forgotten. It was nonetheless finally restored by this Western researcher and writer.

The Source Is Our Human Nature

Combinations of atoms, with their nuclei and orbiting particles, can be viewed as models of the universe with its whirling solar systems and galaxies. In the same manner, the human body can be seen as a miniature model of the workings of nature. Therefore, by studying the relationships of these five elements in nature, we can learn how to become more natural and balanced beings. By studying the parallels in nature, we can become more conscious of our potential for engaging personal power in life.

The five elements that appear as physical matter in and around us are also paralleled in the aspects of the personality. We all move in and out of one element of influence to another. We refer to the effects of changing consciousness as our "moods." The ancient Asian esoteric spiritual sciences describe these influences with a pattern of feelings, physical body centers related to glandular functions, and color associations.

Earth (Stability)

At the earth level, the base of the elemental progression, we are conscious of our solid physicality and stability. We feel a resistance to any change or movement. We desire to maintain things exactly as they are.

We all want to be important. We have a sense of the need to take charge, and command others. When our personality is under the influence of this earth element, we are concerned with keeping things in their places.

The solid element is said to have its center at the base of the spine, way down in the hips, and extends down the legs. In the Himalayan esoteric tradition, the color yellow is associated with this "grounded" physical influence. Rocks are perhaps the most characteristic example of the earth principle. They are incapable of growth, movement, or change without the aid of the other elements.

Water (Flexibility)

At the water level of our physical personality, we are conscious of our own ever changing responses to external stimuli. Water is reflected in the fluid elements of the body.

We all want to know the truth. When our personality is under the influence of this water element, we react to what we encounter. This level of consciousness is characterized by reactions to changes, and adaptability to our surroundings. We are oriented toward the heavier emotions that characterize the self as something separate from all else.

The fluid element is said to have its center in the lower abdomen, what we commonly refer to as the "pit of the stomach." The color blue is traditionally associated with this responsive influence. Plants provide the clearest example of the water principle in action. Plants are capable of independent movement, they react to stimuli, and yet they are incapable of controlling their environment.

Fire (Intensity)

At the fire level, we are conscious of our aggressive nature. Aggression in this sense refers to expansive energy; it is not intended to carry a negative or violent connotation. At this level of consciousness, we experience feelings of warmth, enjoyment, and control over our environment.

We all want to express who we are. We want to express our respect and affection for others, and have them respond in kind to us. When our personality is under the influence of the fire element, we are aware of our connection with our surroundings, and our reasoning faculties.

The fire element is said to be centered at the lower tip of the breast bone, the location we commonly refer to as our solar plexus. The color red is traditionally associated with this expansive, out-going influence. Wild animals are perhaps the most characteristic example of the fire principle. They are capable of remembering and thinking, seeking pleasure, and exerting control over the quality of their lives.

Wind (Flexibility)

From the wind level of our personality, we are aware of our own freedom to move and choose. This influence manifests itself in the desire to serve and to support harmony.

We all want to be part of something bigger than ourselves. We want to serve something that inspires us, something worthy of us. When our personality is under the influence of the wind element, we experience freedom, acceptance, and conscious consideration of our interactions with other individuals.

The wind or air element has its center at the heart in the middle of the chest between the arms. The color green relates to this influence. Human beings are the highest example of the wind principle. They are capable of abstract intellectual understanding and independence from the limitations of the environment.

Creativity Potential

The very middle of the other four quadrants of physical elements is known as *ku*. Difficult to define outside its Eastern context, this is best described as the "great emptiness of *formless potential*." Originally translated by Western scholars as "ethereal substance," this empty or void of specific form energy is today best represented by the concept of subatomic structure. Invisible bits of energy form atoms, which then combine to form the molecules that give base to the entire range of material things.

We all want to experience living up to our highest potential. In our personal make up, this primordial base energy brings about the creative capability to direct the potential through any of the four fundamental elements. *Ku*, the source of all elements, is said to be centered in the throat. The color white is associated with this creative influence.

Recognizable Reflections of the Elements

Your voice takes on the qualities of the five elemental manifestations and inspires precise, though often unconscious, responses in others.

- From the earth center of influence, your voice is heavy, deep, commanding and authoritarian. The lower vibrations of the sound and the full-bodied quality of the tone give the earth voice a solid, grounded feeling.
- Under the influence of the water level of consciousness, your voice becomes husky, sexy, or emotional. In extreme form, the water voice is a gut-level whisper, heard by others as either ominous or seductive.
- From the fire level, your voice is warm, mirthful, and enthusiastic, with a happy attractive tone to it. Terror or hysteria can also take your voice to the rapid and straight-from-the-heart fire quality.
- Under the wind influence, your voice is in the higher, softer registers,

and has a soothing tone to it. Hypnotic, lilting, almost disembodied, the wind voice disarms and calms.

When your vocal expression does not match your body's center of influence, confusion or suspicion develops in your listener. Your ulterior motives show through. Even in untrained listeners, a subconscious awareness produces a sense that something is not right. Your words of love influenced by the water level of personality are interpreted as lust. Your words of command influenced by the water level of personality are interpreted as personal self-interest. Your words of command influenced by the wind level of personality are interpreted as weakness. A thorough knowledge of how your body's centers show up in your voice gives you the ability to "see through" others. You can also learn how to avoid arousing suspicion with your own communications.

Emotional Realities of the Elements

If we examine the five fundamental feelings that are naturally elicited in a threatening situation, we can now see a correlation between our modes of response and the base nature of the elements of our human make-up. We react emotionally from our base in physical nature. Each mode of response to the threat of hostility has its own unique look, flavor, texture, sound, and aroma.

Ninja Shizen no Kamae natural position

Earth (stability)

Under the earth influence in your nature, you hold your ground with strength. Their arguments or fists bounce off you without harm. Like an unmoving mountain with roots deep in the earth, you are the commanding general, firmly maintaining order to repel the encroaching chaos.

Ninja Shizen no Kamae

Ninja Ichi-mon-ji no Kamae Defensive Position

Water (craftiness)

Under the water influence, you reposition for tactical advantage with power. You pull away from their grasp and then hurl yourself back at them from your own angle of access. Like a fluid ocean wave pulling back and building power before crashing forward onto the shore, you are the guerrilla warrior, scientifically and resourcefully frustrating that which would contain you.

Ninja Ichi-mon-ji no Kamae

Ninja Ju-mon-ji no Kamae Aggressive Position

Fire (intensity)

Under the fire influence, you take control of the energy of the process. You invade and cut them down in their tracks before they even know what hit them. Like a flame-thrower leaping out at its target, you are the shock trooper, flying into the face of your adversary at the very moment he begins to suggest a confrontation.

Ninja Ju-mon-ji no Kamae

Ninja Hira no Kamae Evasive Position

Wind (evasiveness)

Under the wind influence, you shift out of the way of the damage. You slip their blows and insults and leave them flailing away foolishly at where you used to be. Like the wind that moves effortlessly through the cracks in the walls of an old house, you are the long-range reconnaissance commando, moving invisibly and invulnerably through the heart of the danger that swirls around you.

Ninja Hira no Kamae

Source Potential Creativity

Under the "empty of form" creative influence, you alter the entire dynamic of the threat. They forgot what it was that they wanted to do to you. You use the power of creativity to virtually redefine an entire arena of endeavor. You are the behind-the-scenes voice that broadcasts a short-wave blend of disparagement and welcome to confuse and demoralize the enemy's cold hungry troops. There is no one *kamae* posture that captures this creative element.

Applying the Knowledge

Remember that no one element of influence is inherently better or worse than any other. None is the single best element. None is the worst element. None is more advanced or less advanced.

The more balanced we are, the more readily we recognize some of each of the elements in our own personality. Some people may find one particular element to be dominant over all the rest. Some people may be so unbalanced that barely a vestige of one or more of the other elements appears in their make-up. Every emotion available to you as a human being can be seen as *more or less effective* in any given set of circumstances.

There are, however, those times when a particular emotion may be regarded as negative or positive, based on its *effectiveness for producing desired results.* An emotion can be seen as a positive tool when it provides an effective approach to resolving the difficulty at hand. Conversely, any emotion can be seen as a negative hindrance when it proves to be an ineffective approach to the situation.

These elements of your *physical make-up* are at the same time natural reflections of your *emotional make-up.* We involuntarily project what we are. We may learn little behavioral cover-up tricks, but at base level we are what we are. The closer we come to danger, the more likely we are to forget all the tricks we have taught ourselves. Our physical disposition reveals itself as an emotional response. Our emotional disposition colors and directs our intellectual processing. These various aspects of us as complex thinking and feeling action machines are all "wired in together" in complete integration. You can not arbitrarily separate one aspect from the other.

It is important to begin with a look at how and why you honestly feel the way you feel when you perceive yourself to be in a hostile situation. All pretense, posturing, and learned cover-ups aside, what do you really sense? That first spark of feeling is what you want to identify, whether the threat is a personality conflict that endangers your job, or a confrontation with a mugger who may want more than walking away with your wallet.

Cunning adversaries will try to lead you one way in order to surprise you from another direction. They will elicit from you an emotional response and then goad you to create your very own defeat through over-reacting. Therefore, it becomes crucially important to be able to recognize and identify your own emotional routines before an enemy can take advantage of your momentum towards loss of self-control.

Five Elements as a Basis for Living

Beyond combat, the five elements describe five ways of reacting based on inner feelings. These quintessential ("five essence") reactions are the grandparents of all personal emotional responses. From the five basic orientations in life stem all the variations in perceptions and behavior.

The five elements capture the ways in which we approach life. Generally, each of us will gravitate towards a particular take on how life works, based on one of the five elements. We are born with a propensity to see life a certain way. We interpret our experiences from this leaning based on one of the five elements.

Coming to grips with such an acknowledgement can be difficult. You really have to want to cut through and expose all your standard routines. You will have to be willing to admit things that you might not want to acknowledge. We are trained to see ourselves as we would *like to be*, rather than the way we really appear to the world. We pretend that since we do not see the real us, everyone else must also be fooled by the mask we don as a disguise.

From an acknowledgement of how your feelings naturally arise when you find yourself in danger, you can condition yourself to utilize those feelings to get the results you need. Allow yourself the authentic emotion, but do it in an effective way that will serve your greater interests.

PART 2

The Elements of Fighting

CHAPTER 3

Earth Ground Holding—*"I Am the Strength of the Earth"*

You may respond by holding your ground. You shore up and defend the space you occupy. You protect your territory and repel invaders.

The ground-holding power-exertion of the earth element shows up as the opposite of the free-moving evasive wind element, which will be described in Chapter 6. From the earth element of influence, you are solid on your feet, dominating space, solidly repelling any attempt to fool you. Begin your training with an exploration of the Chi no Kata "solidity of the earth."

The earth influence is associated with stability, directness, authority, and abundance of strength. You will come to see how this is the exact opposite of wind mobility. What if your attacker moves erratically, in and out of range? You certainly cannot beat his movement. You need a strategy that will focus on your strength and ability to stop him dead.

Theme—*Vision Produces Strength*

The primary earth motivation is the need for stability. We want to stand on our own two feet and set and maintain boundaries. The earth element reminds us of how good it feels to be in charge of our lives and enjoy a sense of down-to-earth fullness. We want to feel important. We want to make our own decisions and create our own benefits in life. We seek abundance. We want to build something of value.

The earth element influence produces people who are moved by confidence in personal belief and an ability to lead. This can, however, produce people who work so hard at building a foundation that they forget the value of an open mind ready for new possibilities.

In its most positive manifestation, this is a noble, magnanimous, generative, and commanding personality, inspiring others to greatness and abundance. People under the earth influence believe in their own intrinsic self worth. They never doubt that they are worthy of the highest and broadest of life's gifts. This is not necessarily a need to impress others, but more of an ability to lead and generate abundance.

Positive Earth "Commander"

The positive earth element inspires leaders, commanders, and executives whose vision inspires the direction of all. Like the heroes of mythology and legend, when we are under the influence of the earth element we are far too big for anything to cause us worry, defensiveness, or fear. The earth element influence is also the ground of the "earth mother" type; solid, reassuring, and strong, ever there for loved ones and reliable in any crisis.

Positive earth sometimes produces what is referred to as majesty. As history-making leaders, they inspire progress girded by stability. As command generals, they bring out willingness to take on the worst of challenges. As visionary monarchs, they touch hearts with their broadness of vision and care for all. Veritable mountains of strength and nobility, such persons seem impervious to fear or doubt.

The positive orientation towards abundance becomes a form of wisdom. A sense of richness just naturally sees the positive values in any encounter, and can utilize every situation to generate to fruition that which must be. *Grounded, confident, generative,* and *authoritative* would be words typically used by others in describing a "positive earth" type.

Negative Earth "Controller" and "Tyrant"

In its most negative form, earth element influence results in a self-centered and arrogant personality, narrow-minded and scornful of new things, persons, or ideas. *"I see two sides to every argument - my side and the wrong side,"* sums up this outlook. The lower the negative earth influence, the more tendency to resist or push back against factors that threaten an established sense of self identity. Like a stick-in-the-mud, we resist progress even to the point of holding on to the familiar long after it has outlived its usefulness. Therefore, ever greater is our need to control others in order to resist change.

The *weak* negative earth influence produces the whiner who controls others through the kind of exaggerated stubborn weakness that engenders feelings of pity or a sense of guilt in others. We feel compelled to take over and do it for the "weak earth" person. That is exactly how they get their way.

The *strong* negative earth element inspires the cruel dictator tyrant, whether head of a country or just running the branch office. Negative earth also creates the tight-fisted school principal who knows all, particularly the importance of strict discipline, order, and protocol. This may appear as unquestioning assertion of authority, the police mentality of, "I just enforce the laws; I don't make them." Learning new skills is difficult because new ideas cause us to challenge things that brought previous successes.

As a limitation, the earth personality can easily get caught up relating only to that which produces a sense of security, comfort, or rightness. He or she can end up immobilized by the weight of all that is carried along. We can become so committed to command and control that we fail to see the value of any new thing that could provide for advancement. *Stubborn, arrogant, narrow-minded*, and *egotistical* would be words typically used by others in describing a "negative earth" type.

Negative Expression	**Positive Expression**
Complacent	Seeing the value of what we have
Demanding	Confident
Repressed	Conservative
Dictatorial	Commanding
Self-centered	Appreciating personal abundance

The mandala symbol for the earth element is the *chinta-mani* "wish-fulfilling gem." In western symbolism, this might be represented by the cornucopia horn of plenty, or the jeweled crown of the monarch. Source of limitless abundance, the earth influence is further symbolized by the color golden yellow and placed in the south in relation to the other elements.

How This Shows Up in Unarmed Combat

Have you gained the skill of *taking a position for strength* instead of engaging his speed or timing? The greater lesson is how to maintain your position in order to dominate and negate his choices.

Some people mistake this for "freezing" or "immobilization." This is not at all an accurate interpretation. You are actually making him have to deal with your strength. A parallel would be fighting a group of snappy little dogs. Would you jump around and try to beat the dogs' mobility? Or would you be better off crouching low and kicking them as they moved here and there?

Have you gained the skill of *stopping the adversary's technique?* You close the gap and apply strong strikes or leverage to beat him down? The greater lesson is how to move against what is thrown at you in such a way as to completely shut down his advance.

Have you gained the skill of *angling to thwart his defense* instead of accommodating his movements? The greater lesson is how to make him uncomfortable and force him to reposition for best placement. While he is moving, you shut him down with direct attacks.

"Earth" Foundational

Here is an example of the most basic ninja earth "holding your ground" approach.

1

2

1. Aggressor approaches you antagonistically. You lift your hands and maintain your position from the ninja's *shizen-no-kamae*.
2. Aggressor suddenly lurches forward, knocks your hands up...

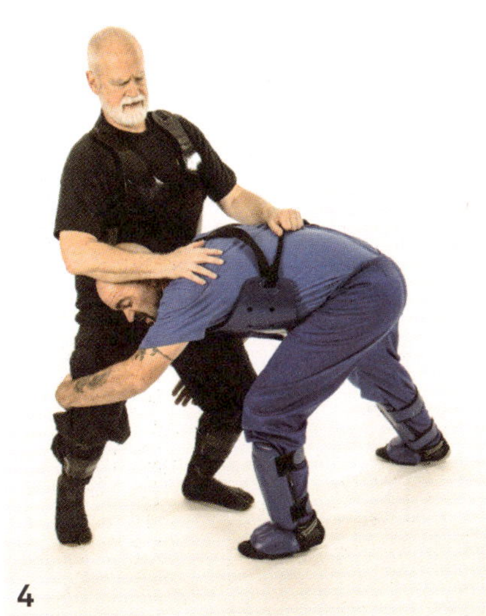

3. …and drops down for a double leg takedown.
4. Keep your back straight, drop your hips, and pull your leg back.

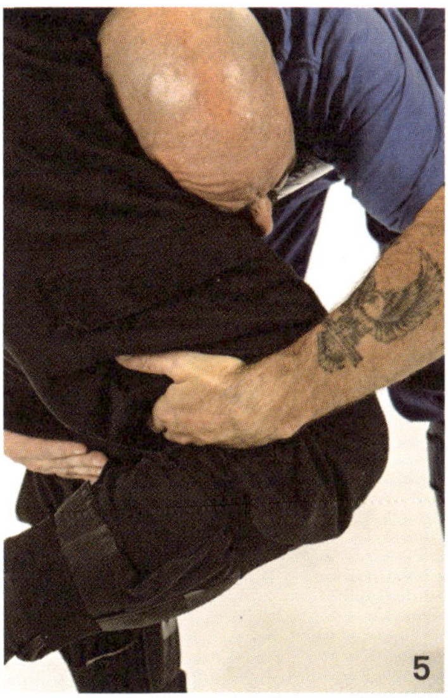

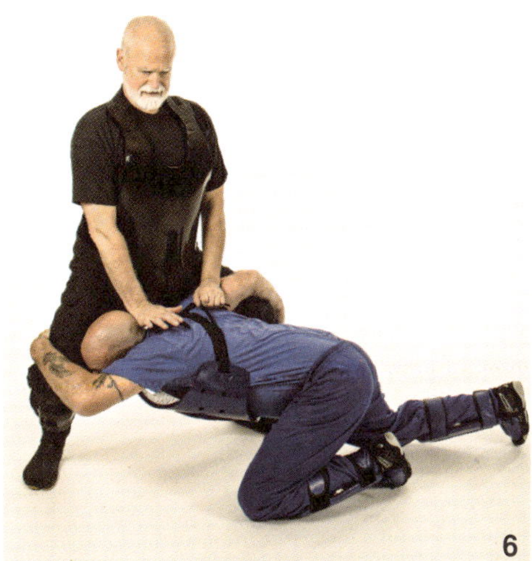

5. Trap his hand in the fold of your knee if possible.
6. Slam down on his shoulders to immobilize him.

"Earth" Solid Strike Defense inside Heavy Hook Punch

1

2

1. Aggressor approaches you antagonistically. Sink into a rooted stance with your knees flexed, back straight, and hands up in the center of your chest.
2. As the attacker suddenly throws a right punch around your defending hands, sink down slightly, and drive your right fist edge into the right side of his neck as you grab and pull his moving right hand.
3. Pull his right arm down across your stomach and continue to push up and out on his neck.
4. Step forward with your left foot and knock his right shoulder back.
5. Step with your right foot to take him to the ground on his back, while maintaining an upward pull on his right arm to hold him in place.

3

4

5

"Earth" Knee Counter to Low Kick

1. Sink into a rooted stance with your knees flexed, back straight, and hands at your hips.
2. As the attacker suddenly throws a low kick to your knee or thigh....

1

2

3

4

3. ... lift your left foot high to shield yourself.
4. Pull your foot back, perhaps hooking his kicking leg, as you throw a left punch to his sternum in the center of his chest.
5. As he falls away, either as a result of your hit or because he is protecting himself, throw a right punch to his throat.

5

"Earth" Leg Trap Pulldown

1. Aggressor dumps you on the ground and stands over you with slaps or punches.
2. Lift your right leg up...

3. ...and around attacker's left leg.
4. Kick his right leg with your left leg to destabilize him.

5

6

5. Grab his left arm and pull forward while pushing out with your left foot.
6. Throw him to the ground.

7

8

7. Kick him repeatedly in the head and make your escape, or you could wrap your arm around his ankle…
8. …and then straighten up to dislocate his ankle.

CHAPTER 4

Water Tactical Positioning—*"I'll Find My Way In"*

In this book I build on the success-generation principles of personal confidence, ability to recognize potential danger, and capacity to respond effectively that you learned through the book *The Ninja Defense*. Beyond grounded "earth-strong" stability and command, you now explore more elemental possibilities.

The tactical and strategic movement of the water element shows up as the opposite of the intercepting direct fire element, which will be described in Chapter 5. From the water element of influence, you shift, angle, and move on your feet, confusing any attempt to dominate you.

The water influence is associated with strategy, indirectness, self-relating, and moving power. You will come to see how this is the exact opposite of fire directness. What if your attacker moves quickly, directly invading your position? You certainly cannot move faster than his initial movement. You need a strategy that will focus on your cleverness and ability to confound him.

Theme – Knowledge Leads to Power

Sui no Kata water element dynamics are the tactics of *power and knowledge, self-discovery, strategy, and individuality*. This is the cool science of learning secrets for success. You apply disciplined training to develop your skills. You learn to use strategic timing, distancing, and positioning to win against an aggressive invasive attacker.

The water element reminds us of how good it feels to know what is really true about life, clearly see what our personal strengths and weaknesses are, and ultimately come from a place of inner natural knowing.. The primary water motivation is the need to know and understand. We want to know the truth about "what's what." We want to know that we are right. We want to believe we see things as they truly are, regardless of what we might hope things to be. We want to know who we are and who we are meant to be. We seek clarity. We want to know all the secrets of life.

The water element influence produces people who are idea oriented and seeking new options, innovations, and concepts, but who may quest so deeply for answers that little concern is given to social considerations.

In its most positive manifestation, this is a scientific self-determining personality, removed from hopes and fears, coolly observant from a distance, operating from intuitive gut level response. People under the water influence see themselves as truth-seekers and tend toward introversion and reserved but direct speech. This is not necessarily coldness, but more of a need to keep distance between self and others for more clarity, and then effectively relate to truth.

Positive Water "Investigator"

The positive water influence produces scientists, inventors, and trouble-shooters who discover the secrets for turning confusion into clarity. Like the heroes of detective stories and spy novels, when we are under the influence of the water element we use all at hand strategically to meet any challenge. The water element also inspires researchers and explorers who turn generations of dreams and superstitions into knowledge of reality.

Positive water sometimes produces what is referred to as wizardry. As mysterious guides like King Arthur's magician Merlin, Frodo's mentor Gandalf, or Luke Skywalker's teacher Obi-wan, these knowledge bearers show us the way to find our strengths. As genius technicians they change our worlds with their insights and inventions. Such people epitomizing the water influence can appear enigmatic, secretive, and powerful.

The positive orientation to scientific knowledge becomes a form of wisdom in which any given situation or encounter is seen clearly as though reflected in a mirror without emotional biases or prejudices. We can grasp the way to bring into clarity that which must be. *Strategic, clever, scientific* and *knowledgeable* would be words typically used by others in describing a "positive water" type.

Negative Water "Schemer" and "Mad Scientist"

In its most negative form, this water element results in an isolated personality, cold and cut off from all concern for others, even seeing all others as potential opposition. People characterized by the negative water influence are often hard to get to know. They feel distance is safety, whether in terms of social, physical, or cultural differences. Change advocated by others is embraced only as long as it is perceived to be to one's own strategic or tactical advantage.

Weak negative water inspires the "office schemer," the sneaky trickster out to topple those who have bettered him, and preferably in a manner in which the victims don't even realize what has happened. We feel confused by their jargon and misdirection, and assume they know what they are talking about. That is exactly how they get their way.

Strong negative water is characterized by the mad scientist who creates a monster through lack of human considerations. Negative water also creates the antisocial hermit genius who willfully uses technology to threaten or destroy life. This may appear as cold self-determined values being inflicted on others to force into being personally held rationalizations about how things "should be." Dealing with people is difficult for these types because they are frustrated by how others "just don't get it."

As a limitation, the water personality can easily get caught up in relating only to that which brings knowledge, even at the cost of lack of effectiveness or never achieving their true purpose. We can become so involved with information that it obscures our perspective rather than assist us in better defining our position. *Defensive*, *aloof*, *cold*, and *scheming* would be words typically used by others in describing a "negative water" type.

Negative Expression	Positive Expression
Distant	Empirical
Angry	Adamant
Manipulative	Tactical
Selfish	Committed
Intellectually fixed	Knowledgeable

The mandala symbol for the water element is the vajra "indestructible diamond thunderbolt," cool and crystal clear like the best of scientific investigation. From Western symbolism, the open book of knowledge or the laboratory test tube could represent this value. The essence of timeless unconditioned truth, the water influence is further symbolized by the color deep sky blue and placed in the east in relation to the other elements.

How This Shows Up in Unarmed Combat

In addition to tool development exercises utilizing training targets and shadow-boxing for physical conditioning and refinement of technique, you practice semi-free *randori* sparring—working with others to simulate how to recognize an attack and coming up with just the right counter.

Each lesson you experience in Ninja Survival To-Shin Do teaches:

1. A *specific technique* for protecting against an aggressor in a self-defense situation.
2. A focused *conditioner* for developing a particular mind and muscle strength.
3. A comprehensive *tactic* that relates to generating success in other similar situations.
4. An underlying *strategy* that relates to handling greater forms of challenge in life.
5. A universal *principle* for insight into actualizing your highest potential.

Have you gained the skill of *moving off the line of attack* at an angle to protect vulnerable areas while opening the assailant's vulnerabilities at the same time? The greater lesson is how to recognize the real problem and reposition yourself so you are not so vulnerable. You find a position to more successfully resolve the problem.

Some people mistake this for "backing up" or "backing off." This is not at all an accurate appraisal. You are actually repositioning for even more advantage. A parallel would be fighting a shark in deep water. Would you attack the shark directly with a punch to the teeth, or would you be better off angling away from the teeth and attacking the shark's gills?

Have you gained the skill of using flexed-knee *angular footwork* to increase stability and power while positioning where the aggressor cannot fully utilize his power? The greater lesson is how to use unexpected strength and approaches that are not usual methods for problem solving.

Have you gained the skill of using fluid *retreat-and-return* "ocean wave crash-back" action to generate knockdown leverage? This counters the aggressor's attempts at timing. The greater lesson is how to recognize and take best advantage of who you are and where you are to trick the problem into a position where you can overcome it.

"Water" Foundational

Here is an example of the most basic water "tactically positioning" approach.

1. Aggressor approaches you antagonistically. You lift your hands and pull strategically away from him, assuming the ninja's *ichimonji-no-kamae*.
2. As he approaches, you angle right with your back straight and weight on your rear leg.
3. He throws a left straight punch, which you slip to the outside with a right swatting hit.

1

2

3

4

5

4. Push back against his left arm with your left fist.
5. Rock back in with a right palm heel slam to the side of his head.

"Water" Outward Rolling Defensive Strike to Incoming Punch

1. Attacker invades your space to punch or grab
2. Pull back to Defensive Posture as he advances on you. As he throws an exploratory left straight punch, smack it over with your right palm.
3. Shift or step back (to his inside) with an outward-rolling defensive hand-edge or fist hit to his punching/shoving arm. This is a forceful and damaging strike, not a passive block or cover.
4. Rock in with the same hand as a punch or palm to face or throat.

1

5. Shift forward with a cross hand punch or palm to the head or chest.
6. Swing up a right groin kick.
7. Trap him and take him down as he responds to the groin kick.

2

3

4

5

6

7

"Water" Inward Rolling Defensive Strike to Incoming Punch

1

2

1. Aggressor approaches you antagonistically. You lift your hands and pull strategically away from him.
2. He throws a right cross punch, which you slip to the outside with a left swatting hit.

3

4

3. Rock back in with a right palm heel slam to the side of his head.
4. Send your rear leg out…

5. ...with a stamping kick to his leg.
6. Catch his trapped arm with inward elbow pressure.

5

6

7. As he pulls his arm back to get it loose, allow your right hand to fly forward with a clawing finger face catch.
8. Spin your left leg back and around to unbalance him and take him to the ground.

7

8

"Water" Punch-Deflecting Defense on Ground – Shadowboxing and with Partner

1. From the floor on your back, the aggressor between your knees throws a right punch to your face.
2. Shift your hips right and face left, and knock his punch away with an outward roll of your right arm.
3. Aggressor between your knees throws a left punch to your face.

1

2

3

4

5

4. Shift your hips left and your face right, and knock his punch away with an outward roll of your left arm, lifting your right leg high along his left ribs.

5. Roll back to your right and jam his left arm into a face-down elbow bar.

6

7

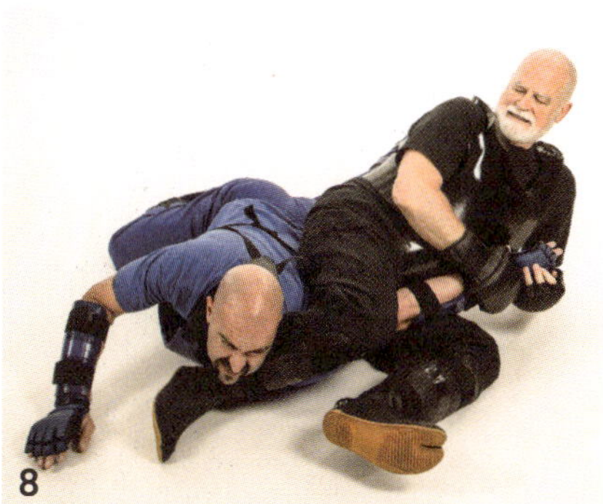

8

9

6. Throw your foot in front of his face.
7. Hook his left shoulder with your right leg.
8. Pull his left arm back as you sit up.
9. Lie back to dislocate his shoulder.

"Water" Defense against Sideways Headlock Attack (next page)

1. Aggressor squares up and starts his attack.
2. Aggressor tries to grab your neck in a headlock. Crouch and brush your forearms overhead to move his arm away.
3. Push his left arm across his mid-section…
4. …and strike to his ribs to knock him back.
5. If he does get you in a headlock…
6. …flex your knees, "horse-bite" grab with your fingertips his left thigh and reach up over his back, use your hand-edge to the bottom of his nose to force him back.

1
2
3
4
5
6

7. Be sure to maintain your stability as you grab. Do not hunch forward into his grip.
8. Jam your little finger up and into his nose.

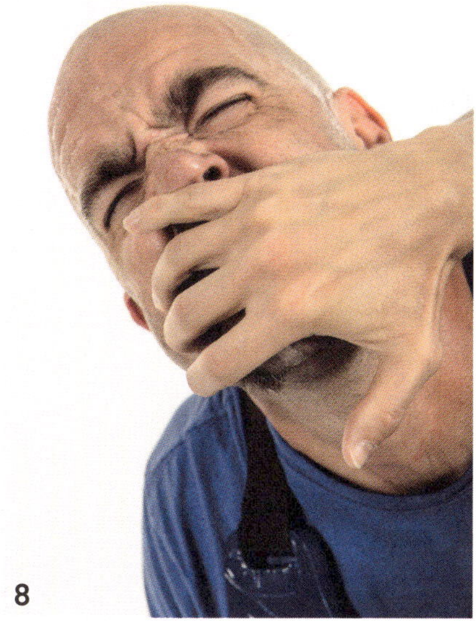

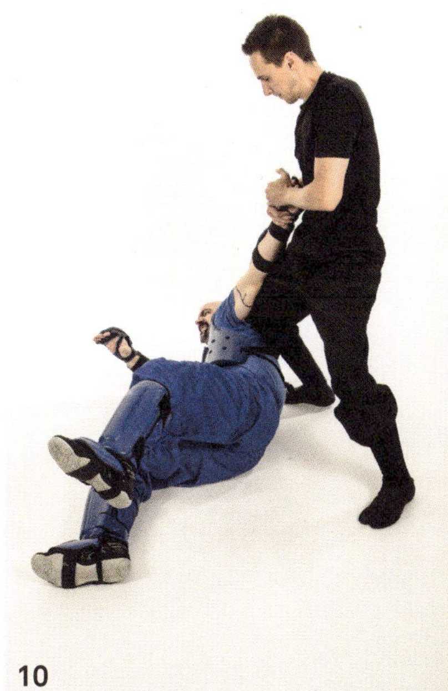

9. Grab the skin of his inner thigh and pull up on his leg and push down and back on his nose to dump him on the ground.
10. Drop him to the ground with a shoulder projection lock on his left arm.

"Water" Wrist Twist Response to a Hair Grab

1. Aggressor grabs you by the hair from behind with his right hand...
2. ...and pulls you backwards.
3. Straightening your back, cover his hand with both of yours and press his hand into your scalp firmly.
4. Shift back with your left foot and turn left as you push your right shoulder forward toward the attacker.
5. Keep your back straight and step back under his right arm.

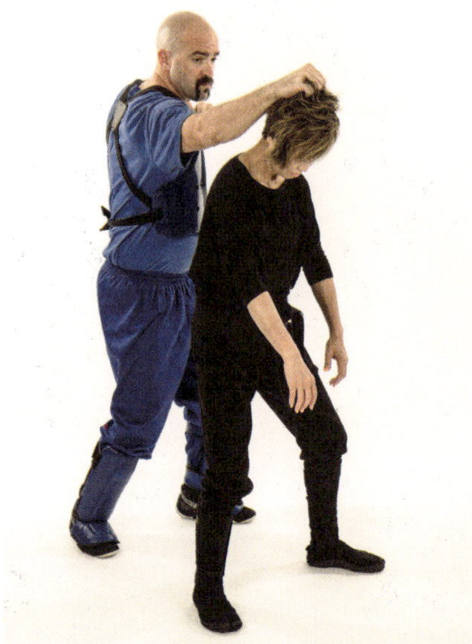

1

2

3

4

5

6

7

6. Continue to turn to your left, holding his hand in place, locking up his right arm.
7. Repeat the turning step to your left if necessary to lock up his arm. Peel his hand away and pull out on his arm as you push back with your left hand.

"Water" Defensive Angling Response to Incoming Grab Pressure

1. Recognize the attack as his hand grabs your wrist with a cross grab shove.
2. Pull your trapped hand side back. Move the whole side of your body...
3. ...and palm-heel his elbow to dislodge his grip.
4. Switch your gripping hand to hold him in place momentarily.

1

2

3

4

5

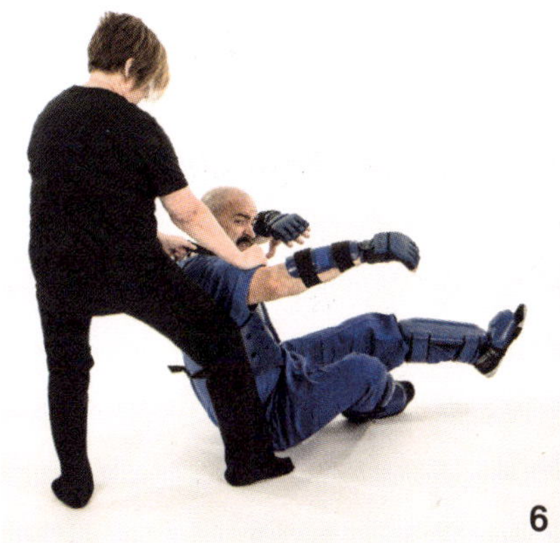

6

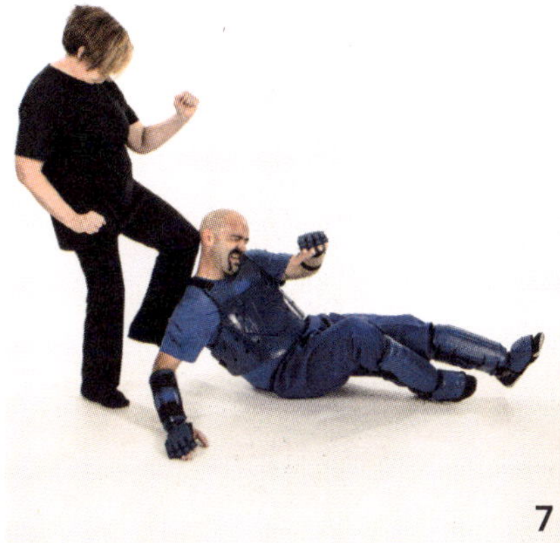

7

5. Kick his exposed knee with heel stamp kick.
6. Maintain your backward pull…
7. … and knee him in the back of the head as he falls over.

Defense against Around-the-Waist Bear-Hug under the Arms

1. Aggressor grabs under your arms and pulls you into a rear bear hug.
2. Swing your left elbow back at his head…
3. …and then a right elbow strike, so that he is distracted as you prepare to…
4. …pull forward…

1

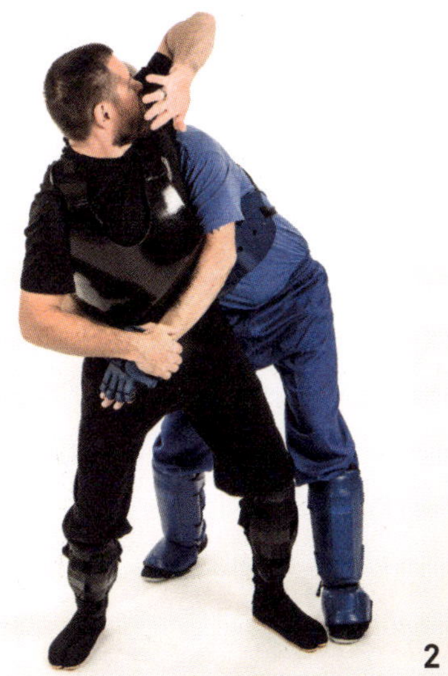

2

3

4

5. ...and drive your hips back and grind your elbow into his elbow.
6. Pull to the side of the arm you are drilling.
7. Peel his hands apart.
8. Step out, turn around, and twist his wrist in towards the center of his body.

5

6

7

8

9

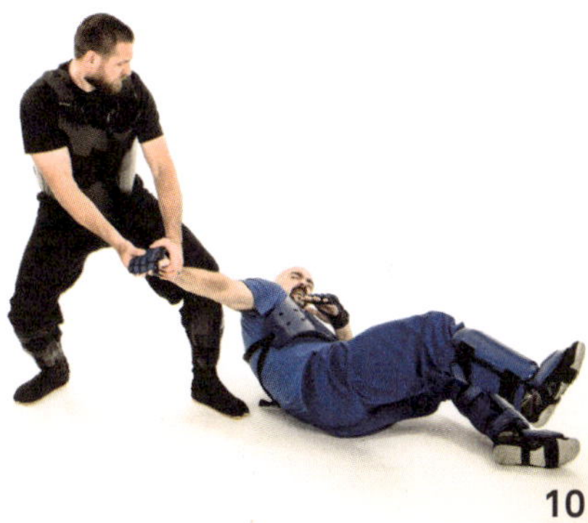

10

9. Step back and continue to twist his straightened arm.
10. Flip him over onto his back and jam his shoulder with your left knee.

Defense against Around-the-Waist Bear-Hug over the Arms

1. Aggressor grabs over your arms and pulls you into a rear bear hug.
2. Shift your hips to the right and swat his groin with your left hand while applying a rear head butt.

1

2

3

4

3. Grasping his hand, lift his trapped arm over your head.
4. Drop to your right knee and pull him forward over your shoulder.
5. Pull his arm across your front…
6. …throwing him onto his back.

5

6

"Water" Defensive Strike and Kick Response to Jacket Grab

1. Aggressor moves forward with threats and you strategically angle back.
2. Aggressor grabs your jacket with his left hand and punches to your face with his right.

1

2

3

4

3. Pin his left hand and angle back and away with a left hammer fist strike to his face or right arm.
4. Drive forward with a right palm heel strike to the face.
5. Kick his right thigh with a left stamp…
6. …and knock his right leg back.

5

6

7. Kick behind his left thigh or knee with a right lateral shin kick…
8. … to knock him down.
9. If he still holds on, back away to straighten his arm…
10. …and knock the hand away

7

8

9

10

CHAPTER 5

Fire Preemptive Attack—*"I Nailed It!"*

In a third possibility, Hi no Kata fire element dynamics are the energy of *committed intensity and intercepting focus*. You learn to catch a problem as it builds. You intercept at just the right moment. Imagine this as the opposite of the water principle covered in Chapter 4.

Theme—Clinging Becomes Focused Desire Which Leads to Energy

The fire influence shows up as the magnetic power of energy, artistry, relationship, and communication. The fire element reminds us of how good it feels to be connected with our world as a participant. It manifests as the enjoyment-oriented personality.

The primary fire motivation is the need for interconnection between self and others. We all want to be noticed. We want the world to know who we are. We want to tell our story and have it heard. We want to be recognized, acknowledged, respected, appreciated, and loved by others. We want to express our respect, admiration, affection, and love for others.

The fire influence produces connected or outgoing people who measure themselves against external considerations. People influenced by fire are moved by trends and fashion, but seldom take control and make their own statements going against consensus.

In its most positive manifestation, this is a compassionate personality able to empathize and communicate effectively and even artistically with others. People under the fire influence are animated with an intensity of assertiveness and exuberance. They are warm, dynamic, and expansive, using their reasoning powers to control their environment. This is not necessarily a hostile aggressiveness in the sense of needing to dominate, but more of using one's will to succeed and enjoy that success.

Positive Fire ("Communicator Artist")

Positive fire influence produces the artist, the communicator, the lover, or the charismatic leader who attracts followers naturally just by being an attractive person associated with all that others desire or hope for. Fire people pull others into interaction, make others feel good, and are good responsive listeners. Their enthusiasm and animation add excitement or entertainment wherever they go.

Positive fire sometimes produces what is referred to as star quality. As lovers they are addictive. As artists they are captivating. As political figures they are exhilarating. As entertainers they are irresistible. Dynamic performers and speakers and sports stars know how to capture an audience by means of engaging the magnetically seductive power of the fire element.

The positive orientation of energetic passion for connection becomes a form of wisdom in which discriminating awareness just naturally sees precisely the specific characteristics and values of each thing encountered. This discriminating awareness knows how to put them to work judiciously in prompting along to fruition that which must be. *Engaging, entertaining, warm*, and *charismatic* would be words typically used by others in describing a "positive fire" person.

Negative Fire ("Defeatist" and "Performer")

In its most negative form, fire element influence results in a desperately passionate personality driven for acknowledgement from all others, even seeing others' approval as the only key to happiness. Personal worth and self-esteem are tied to external appearance and social status, resulting in a surface involvement in any situation. Some people are so consumed by what other people think that they find it impossible to follow their true calling. With no core identity, everything becomes a reflection of external fads and values. *Shallow*, *aggressive*, *flirty*, and *flighty* are words typically used to describe a "negative fire" type.

Weak negative fire influence produces an overly needy desperately clingy personality who radiates, "I can't make it without you." Weak negative fire can also result in a self-conscious self-defeatist who gives up on ever getting what he craves, and talks himself out of even trying. Zealots crusade with fiery passion against the very thing that tempts them with what they fear they will never get.

Strong negative fire is characterized by the aggressively showy personality who is always "on" and can never relax or be at peace. *"If I am not the center of attention, then something's wrong,"* sums up this outlook. Without a balanced sense of inner worth, these people can easily burn out way ahead of their time. This is typical of the flamboyant entertainment superstar who gains too much success too fast, loses all sense of self, and ends up dead from alcohol or drugs.

As a limitation, the fire influenced personality can easily get caught up in relating only to that which is stimulating. The pizza is never spicy enough, the Ferrari never red enough, the music never loud enough, the lovers never sexy enough. We can so passionately chase possessing to where our compulsive desire spots new targets so fast that we never stop to enjoy what we get.

Negative Expression	**Positive Expression**
Attention-seeking	Self-disclosing
Desperate	Intensely alive
Greedy	Unrestrained
Distracted	In touch with others
Superficial	Entertaining

The mandala symbol for the fire element is the lotus blossom, born of murky water but blooming to bright sunlight, symbolizing the ideal of compassionate connection reaching out. In Western symbolism, fire element icons might be the red rose or red Valentine heart. Fire influence is further symbolized by the color sunset red and placed in the west in relation to the other elements.

How This Shows Up in Unarmed Combat

Have you gained the skill of *generating momentum from centered movement* instead of using crude reactive "push-off" footwork? The greater lesson is how to be in position to take advantage of opportunity the moment it appears. You are ready to take command of the fight.

Some people mistake this for "going crazy" or "charging blindly." This is not at all an accurate appraisal. You are actually tuning into his energy to be ready to respond as his attack starts. An example would be stopping a person from getting out of his chair to fight you. Would you step back to allow him to rise, or would you be better off diving in and keeping him seated and vulnerable to your own attack?

Have you gained the skill of *pre-emptive advancing at the moment the adversary begins* his attack? The greater lesson is how to take charge of the problem soon enough so that the difficulty opposing you does not have time to build strength.

Have you gained the skill of *reading the adversary's movements* so that you know just what he is about to do, even before he does? The greater lesson is how to recognize and take best advantage of what is unconscious "human nature" and then set up the situation in such a way where the difficulty just cannot help but to follow through out of habit.

"Fire" Foundational

Here is an example of the most basic ninja fire "intercepting" approach.

1. You watch and take in every move the aggressor makes.
2. From the ninja's *jumonji-no-kamae*, fire out a lead hand punch the second the aggressor starts his move.
3. Continue forward to catch the aggressor behind the neck...

1

2

3

4. ...and pull him forward with an elbow strike to the face.
5. While he is off-balance, pull your right leg back...

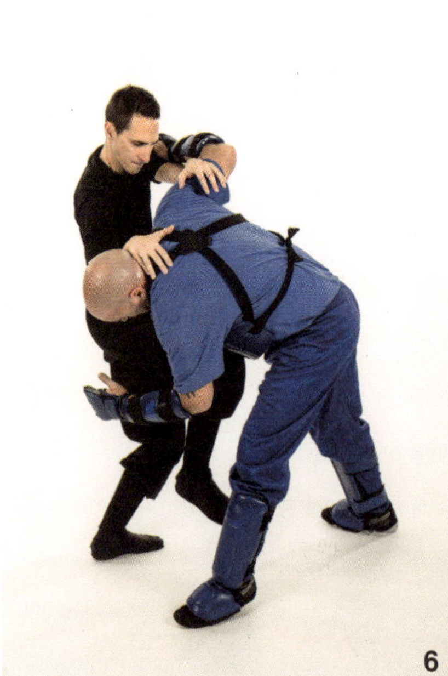

6. ...and then send it forward with a knee to his midsection.
7. Throw him forward away from you.

"Fire" Response to Big Wind-Up Swing Hit; Jam, Hit the Solar Plexus, Throw

1. Advance into attacking fighting posture.
2. Charge into the attacker's right punch or club swing with a left *shuto* hand edge to the neck.

1

2

3

4

3. Pull back with your right arm…
4. ..and hit with cross punch down into the solar plexus.

5

6

5. Shift across in front with a head-butt and push.
6. Push your hip into the midsection and twist to your right with a *gan-seki-otoshi* forward takedown.
7. Finish as appropriate, and resume preemptive fighting posture to defend against the next move.
8. Trap the arm with an elbow bar to control.

7

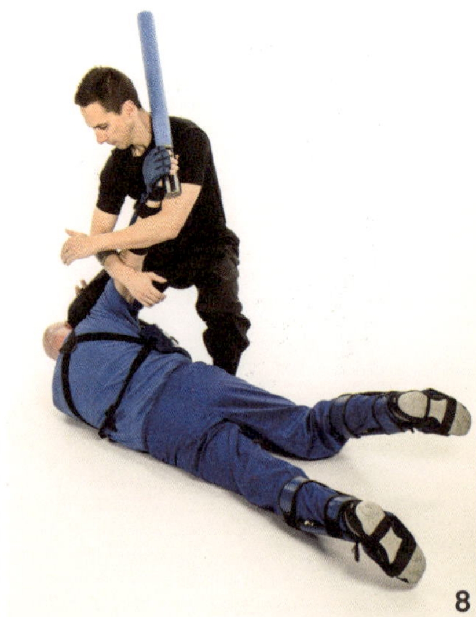

8

"Fire" Interception of Front Kick Attack; Slip Inside, Punch Knee, Back-Knuckle Face

1. Advance into attacking fighting posture.
2. Shift inside (or outside) attacker's front kick...
3. ...with a leading hand punch to his knee as you move forward past his foot.
4. Swing the same fist up with an elbow to his solar plexus...

1

2

3

4

5. ...and then a right backhand strike to his face....
6. ..and then a left punch to the face.

"Fire" Slip and Slap Hit Outside Leading-hand, Follow with Jam and Lift with Punches

1. Advance into attacking fighting posture, watching every move he makes.
2. Slip outside the attacker's leading right hand jab with a left cross outside slap.

3

4

5

6

3. Jam his arm in place...
4. ...and cross punch with your rear fist.
5. Lift your right elbow to hit him in the face and catch his shoulder...
6. ...and step to your left to unbalance him...
7. ... and take him to the ground.

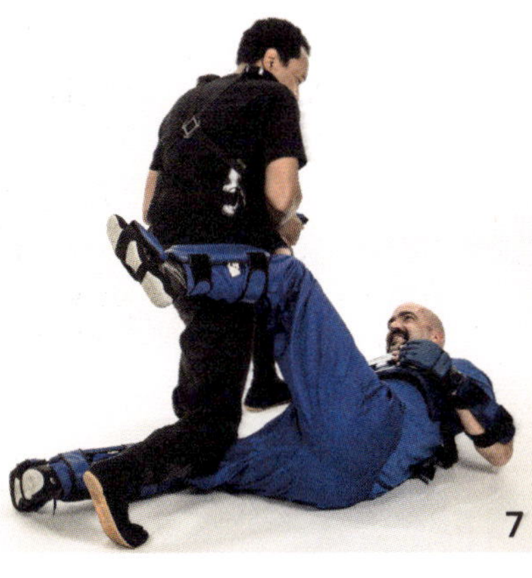

7

Rear Takedown *(Osoto-Gake)*

1. You creep forward, waiting for the aggressor to make his move.
2. Assailant reaches or punches around toward your chest with his right hand.

1

2

3

4

3. Deflect his right arm outward with a left push on the inside of his right forearm.
4. Push his left shoulder back and pull his right shoulder/arm forward.

5. Step past him—your right side next to his—and pull your right foot up...
6. ...to stamp down with a sweep, your right leg behind his right leg.
7. Step forward with your right foot to take him back and down to his seat.

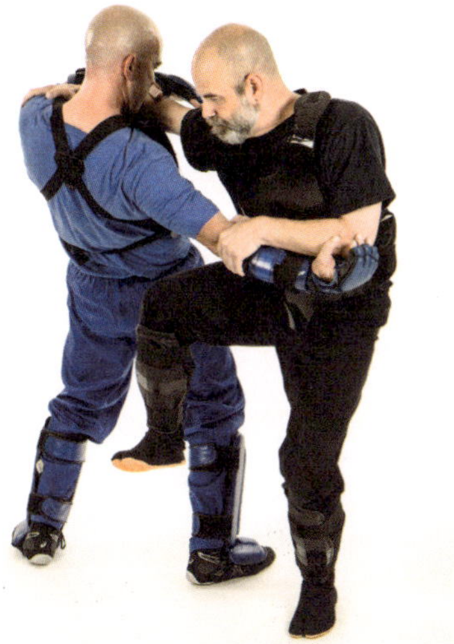

5

6

7

Forward Takedown *(Ganseki-Nage)*

1. You inch forward, waiting for the aggressor to make his move.
2. Assailant reaches or pushes straight toward your chest with his right hand.
3. Deflect his right arm upward with a left push and press down on his left forearm.
4. Step in with your left and shove your right hand up under his left armpit and press down on his right forearm to lock him up.

5. Turn into him (face the same direction as aggressor), tripping him with your leg in front of his legs.
6. Drive your right hip into his midsection. Do not allow any space there.
7. Twist and project forward to send him forward…
8. … and down on his back.

5

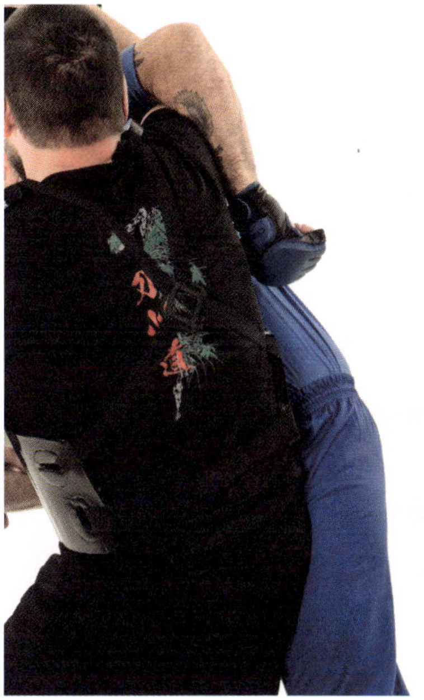

6

7

8

"Fire" Interception of 2-Handed Lapel Grab

1. Recognize 2-handed jacket lapel pulling grab.
2. Slap both his ears forcefully at the same moment.
3. Pull his head in for a head butt to the face.
4. Keep pressure on him as his head recoils from the head butt.
5. Swing a lateral shin kick...

6. ...to buckle his knee.
7. Pull his head tight against your chest.
8. Turn to the rear to pull him to the ground...
9. ... with a twisting throw.

6

7

8

9

Defense from the Ground against Kneeling Attacker

1. Aggressor kneels or crouches next to you on the ground in position to grab, punch, or choke you.
2. Shift to your right hip, tuck your knees to your chest between his arms to shield your body.

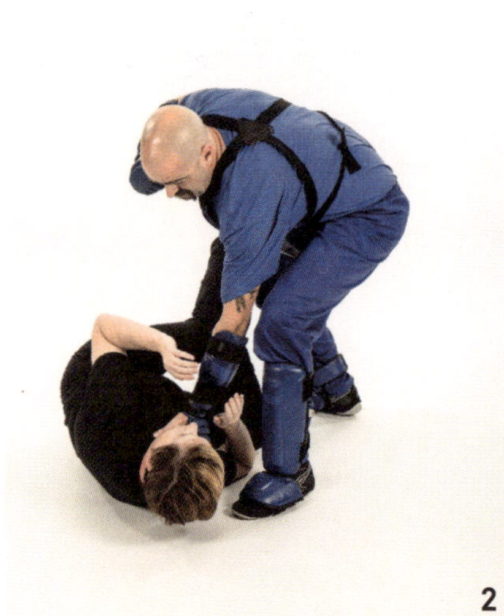

3. Wedge your knees or bottoms of your feet against his chest …
4. …and kick/push him back and away.

5. Quickly roll to your feet to continue your defense.

Defense from the Ground against Standing Attacker

1. Aggressor moves into position to kick or drop down and grab or punch you once you are on the ground.
2. Drive your heel into his stomach or chest.

3. From position on your back, reach beyond the outside of his right leg with your right leg...
4. ...and hook his right ankle with your left ankle to hold his leg in place.

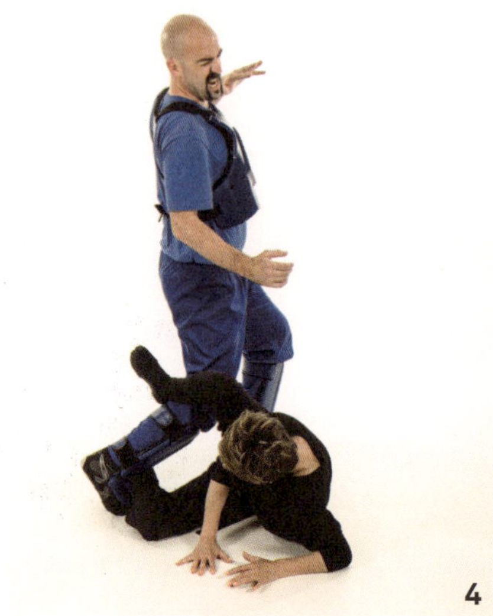

5. Use pushing pressure from your left foot and pulling pressure from your right foot to move him sideways.
6. Kick or lever his leg with your right foot to take him to the ground.

7. Quickly shift to kneeling position on his back to continue your defense.
8. Use a forward lean to maintain pressure on his knee.
9. Keeping his leg trapped, pull back on his head or neck to immobilize him.

7

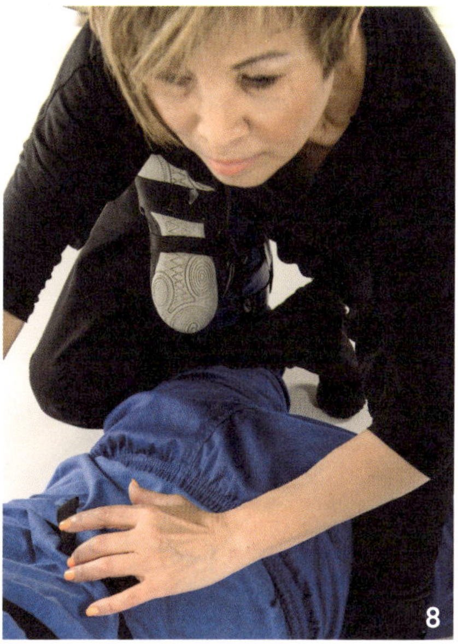

8

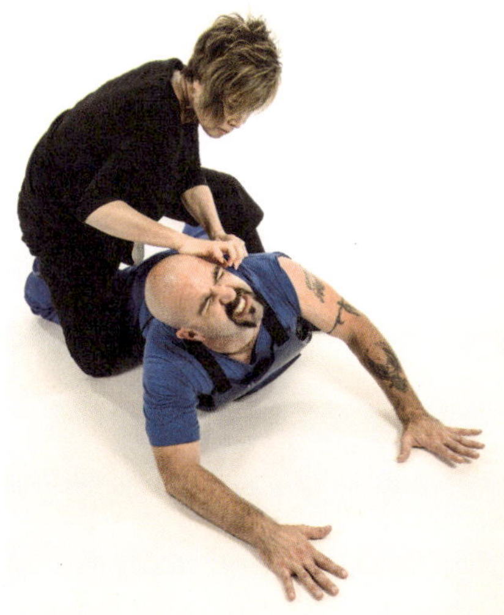

9

CHAPTER 6

Wind Evasive Moving—*"I'm Outa Here"*

The free-moving evasive wind element shows up as an opposite when compared to the ground-holding power-exertion of the earth element described in Chapter 3. From the wind element of influence, you are light on your feet, moving nimbly, deftly evading his attempts to pin you down. Beyond grounded "earth-strong" stability and command, "water power" secret knowledge, and "fire intensity," you now explore a fourth elemental possibility— the Fu no Kata "unpredictability of the wind."

The wind influence is associated with mobility, adaptability, efficiency, and effortless accomplishment. Can you see how this is the exact opposite of earth stability? What if your attacker is too strong to resist, or too determined to beat you? You certainly cannot overpower him. You need a strategy that will allow your weakness to become a way to win.

Theme—*Insecurity Leads to Accomplishing Action*

The primary wind motivation is the need for freedom. We want to be able to change as one thing becomes more important than another. The wind element reminds us of how good it feels to be free to go where we need to be, when we need to be there. We want to serve some cause we feel is worthy of us. We all want to be a part of something grander than us.

The wind element influence produces people who are accomplishment oriented, serving, self-giving, and moved to action by the highest of ideals. This can, however, produce people who may get caught up in relating only to that which produces results, even at cost of others' feelings or missed benefits.

In its most positive manifestation, this is an inspired personality, desiring to serve something greater than self through a conscious consideration of the grander scheme of things. People under the wind influence are ready to change to fit different needs. This is not necessarily insecurity, but more of a willingness to be open to change, embodying unlimited possibilities in the lives of others.

Positive Wind "Server" or "Doer"

Positive wind influence generates law enforcers, social workers, medical professionals, warriors, and educators committed to making the world better. Positive wind people enjoy the dynamic process of achieving as they focus on the challenge of "getting the job done."

The root word for the Japanese *samurai* is *saburau*, meaning, "to serve." The warrior aristocrats of ancient Japan and Europe made private chapel vigil vows of service. They did not make grand public arena promises of victory through violence. Along with protecting the people, the knight was dedicated to good works like charity, education, and aiding the poor and sick. 1950s American cowboy heroes like Hopalong Cassidy and the Lone Ranger stereotype the ideal of protectors who always put others' welfare ahead of their own.

Positive wind sometimes produces what is referred to as saintliness. Heroes selflessly serve a noble cause ahead of their own welfare. They become legends like Joan of Arc, Abraham Lincoln, Mohandas Gandhi, Martin Luther King, Jr., Mother Theresa, and the Dalai Lama.

The positive orientation to action becomes a form of wisdom. Energetic activity just naturally takes the form needed to move along to perfect fruition that which must be. *Generous*, *free*, *efficient*, and *supporting* would be words typically used by others in describing a "positive wind" type person.

Negative Wind "Drifter" or "Compulsive Competitor"

Weak negative wind influence produces the moral drifter who is ready to embrace with temporary fervor every new theory which promises to smooth out the jumbled chaos of life. This results in a rootless and ruthless personality, insecure and therefore secretly competitive. This person is always enmeshed in intrigue, ever abandoning one hope for the next and never really attaining any sense of satisfying completion.

Strong negative wind is characterized by the mercenary or militaristic renegade who takes over when there is a vacuum of leadership. Such a person takes charge when others abdicate. He or she is more than willing to step right in and make things happen for others the way they "should be done." This outlook of sharp efficiency is epitomized by samurai Japan's famed 47 Ronin who sacrificed all for the moment of revenge of their leader's unjust death, in spite of the costs to them and their own families and dependents.

As a limitation, the wind personality can easily get caught up in envy of neighbors' successes. He or she can fall into habitual competitive struggle to win approval of others with a sense of, "As long as I win, people respect me, and if I'm not winning, they have no need for me." The commitment to effectiveness without guidance of vision can become so strong that efficiency becomes our master instead of our servant. *Impatient*, *insecure*, *envious*, and *mechanical* would be words typically used by others in describing the "negative wind" type.

Negative Expression	**Positive Expression**
Fanatic	Inspired
Workaholic	Committed
Ruthless	Unencumbered
Insecure, thus *authority-seeking*	Serving
Competitive	Accomplishing

The mandala symbol for the wind element is the flaming sword that can cut in all directions at once. Efficiently serving the inspiration of the commander, the enlightened warrior's sword symbolizes the ideal of selfless efficient perfect actions in just the right way, place, and time. The essence of freedom of movement which permits being wherever there is need, the wind influence is further symbolized by the color leaf green (or sometimes black) and placed in the north in relation to the other elements.

How This Shows Up in Unarmed Combat

Have you gained the skill of *moving with the aggressor's momentum* instead of resisting his strength or stability? The greater lesson is how to give up your position in order to be in better place to take advantage of the instability that results.

Some people mistake this for "avoiding" or "ducking away." This is not at all an accurate interpretation. You are actually letting go of a position in order to generate best advantage. A parallel would be fighting a dragon in the sky. Would you advance on the dragon directly with an attack to the fire-breathing mouth, or would you duck to the side where the wing would hit you? Or would you be better off evasively securing the neck behind the head?

Have you gained the skill of *proceeding ahead of the adversary's technique*? You provide him the opportunity to get himself in trouble when he expects conventional resistance from you? The greater lesson is how to take best advantage of what is moving against you in such a way as to allow the problem to "become its own solution."

Have you gained the skill of *choosing the appropriate mode of defense* instead of struggling against the movements of his attack? The greater lesson is how to fit into the dynamics of a problem in such a way as to be in the best position to get your way with a minimum of time and effort on your part.

Wind Foundational

Here is an example of the most basic ninja wind "evasively moving" approach.

1. Assume the ninja's *hira-no-kamae* with hands back and apart, moving erratically and lightly on your feet.
2. Rotate to your right and move in to shove his kick away from you.

1

2

3. He ends up unbalanced.
4. Move to position behind him.
5. Slam a push kick with your heel to the back of his left knee to pull him to the ground.

3

4

5

"Wind" Evasive Strike Defense Inside Heavy Hook Punch

1. Rock into evasive fighting posture, on flexed knees and lightly on the balls of your feet in *hira no kamae.*
2. Slip right, inside the attacker's right hook punch…

1

2

3. … with right *happa-ken* open-palm smack to his left ear.
4. Swing your left knee to the right side of his torso under his right punching arm.

3

4

5. Catch his left arm...
6. ... lift up to force him off balance...

5

6

7. ...and spin left away from his punching arm...
8. ... to pull him to the ground.

7

8

"Wind" Evasive Strike Defense Outside Heavy Straight Punch

1. Rock into evasive fighting posture, on flexed knees and lightly on the balls of your feet in *hira no kamae.*
2. Slip outside the attacker's right punch and smack to the right with your left hand and...

1

2

3. ...and hit with right palm heel to the chin.
4. Your right knee can strike his right knee to knock the attacker off balance.

3

4

5

6

7

5. Pull back with right arm hook inside his right shoulder...
6. ...and rotate back and down to your left.
7. Pull him to the ground, and then resume guarded evasive fighting posture in preparation to flee or continue to defend.

Reach under Elbow and Flatten Arm for Rear Shoulder Lock *(Mu-So Dori)*

1. Aggressor advances threateningly.
2. He grabs you by the arms or sleeves of your jacket.
3. Pull your right side back, lifting your hands to disrupt his balance.

1

4. When he tries to pull you back into position, if your hand is on the *outside* of his arm, step forward with your right foot and press your right palm against the back of his left elbow.
5. Push up, inward, and then down to lock his arm out in a flat elbow bar.
6. Apply a hugging elbow lock armbar across your chest from position rising from the ground.

2

3

4

5

6

Reach over Elbow and Scoop Forward Shoulder Lock *(Mu-Sha-Dori)*

1. Aggressor grabs you by the arms or sleeves of your jacket.
2. Step forward with your right foot and reach over his left elbow as far as you can.
3. Swing your right arm down from behind his left elbow.
4. Sink on flexed knees and jam your armpit against the inside of his left elbow.
5. Crouch down, inward, and then up to scoop his arm into a bent elbow lock.
6. Step back to pull him to the ground.

1

2

3

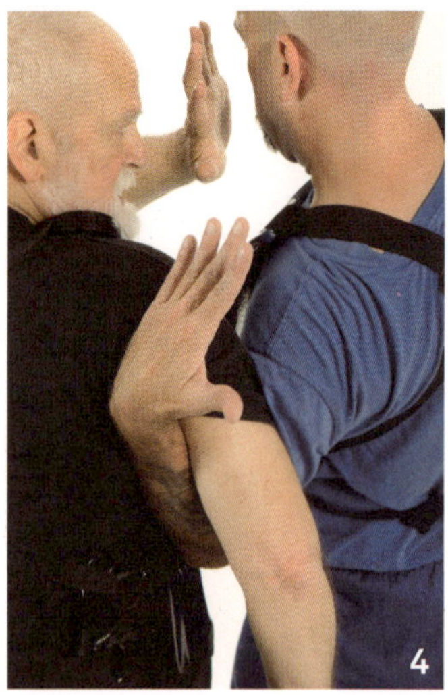

4

5

6

Over-Elbow Pull-Forward Shoulder Lock *(Omote Oni Kudaki)*

1. Aggressor hits at you with a short club.
2. Move in with your right side, elbowing his face and disrupting his balance.

1

2

3. Lock his right arm with your left elbow as you reach over his arm with your right.
4. Step forward and lock your left wrist with your right palm.
5. Pull back, and up to scoop his arm into a bent elbow lock.
6. Pull him backwards to the ground.

3

4

5

6

Under-Elbow Pull-Forward Shoulder Lock *(Ura Oni-Kudaki)*

1. Aggressor moves against you with a short club.
2. Move in with your right side…
3. …elbowing his midsection and disrupting his balance.
4. Lift his right arm with your left forearm as you reach under his arm with your right.
5. Lift his right arm.
6. Step forward with your left foot and lock your right hand on his right wrist.

1

2

3

4

5

6

7

8

7. Pull back, bend your knees low, and rise up to scoop his arm into a bent elbow lock.
8. Take him to the ground.

"Figure 4" Elbow Lift Shoulder Lock with Adversary's Back Flat on Ground *(Oni-Kudaki)*

1. Adversary grabs you behind your neck from his back on the ground.
2. Drop forward with a right elbow to his face.

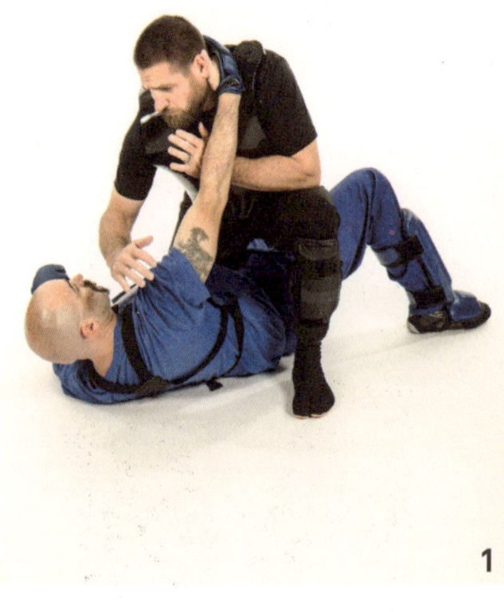

1

2

3. Press against his wrist, and slide your arm under his forearm.
4. Grasp your wrist.
5. Pull up from beneath.
6. Keeping your back straight, lift and twist to dislocate his shoulder.

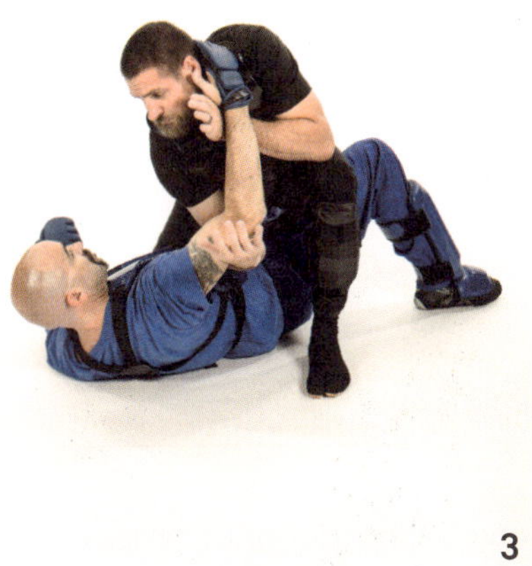
3

4

5

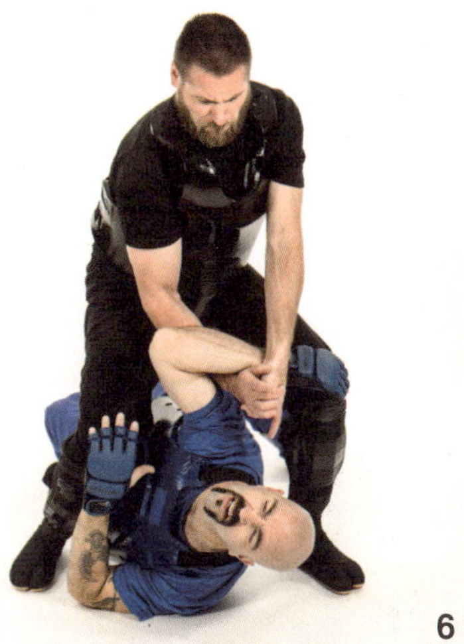
6

Around-Waist Tackle Defense

1. Aggressor charges in from a low position.
2. He knocks your hands up...
3. ...and grabs low behind your knees.
4. As he grabs around your waist with his head beside you, flex your knees to stabilize his force and quickly raise your right hand...

5. ... and smack his ear to break his ear drum.
6. Raise your left hand high...
7. ...and chop down on the back of his neck several times with your hand edge.
8. Wrap your forearm under his neck and hold his head in place with the inside of your arm.

5

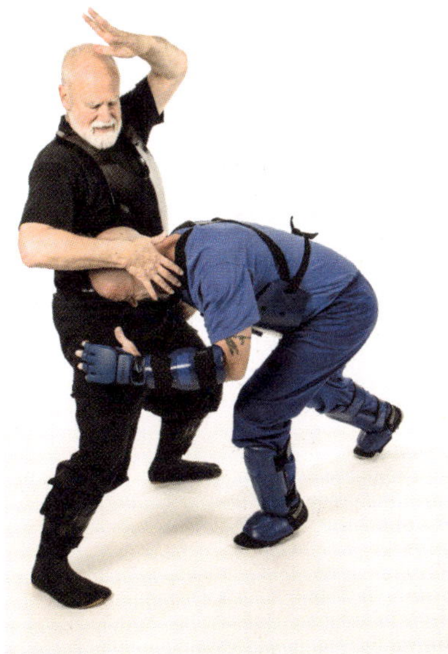

6

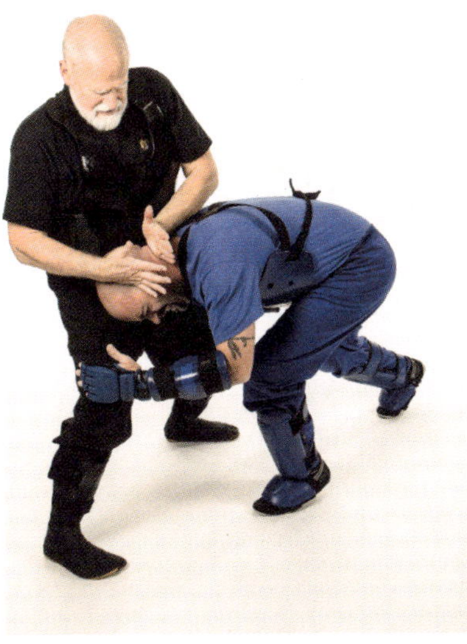

7

8

9. Cause his neck to flex sideways.
10. Pull up to force his chin towards his chest with a "guillotine" action.

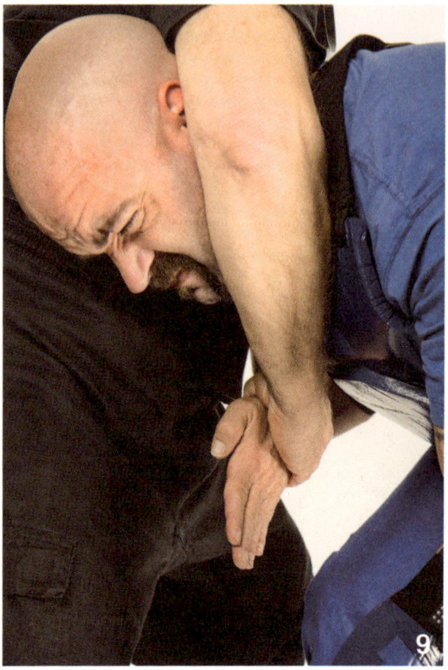

9

10

11

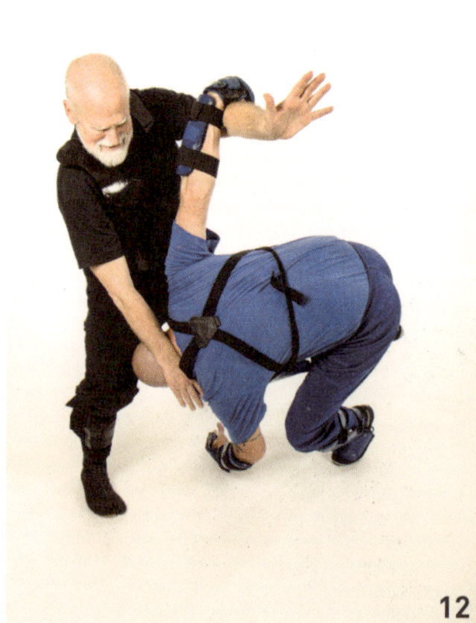

12

11. Lean back to intensify the fold, or advance to lever his arm upwards...
12. ...and throw him over on to his back.

Defense against Rear Choke; Catch Elbow, Drop, Throw over Shoulder *(Ketsu Miyaku)*

1. Aggressor confronts you aggressively.
2. He rushes in...

1

2

3

4

3. ...with grab around your neck.
4. Drive your elbow back into his ribs.

5. Push up and back with your head.
6. Move forward and drop to kneeling position, pulling him forward with you.

5

6

7

8

7. Hug his arm and project your trapped shoulder forward.
8. Throw him over onto his back.

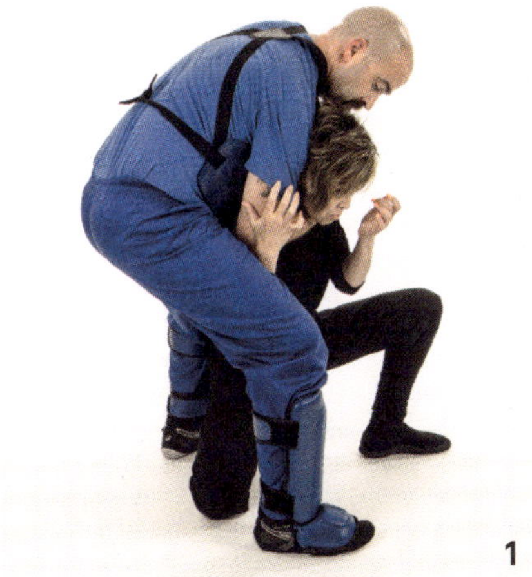

1

2

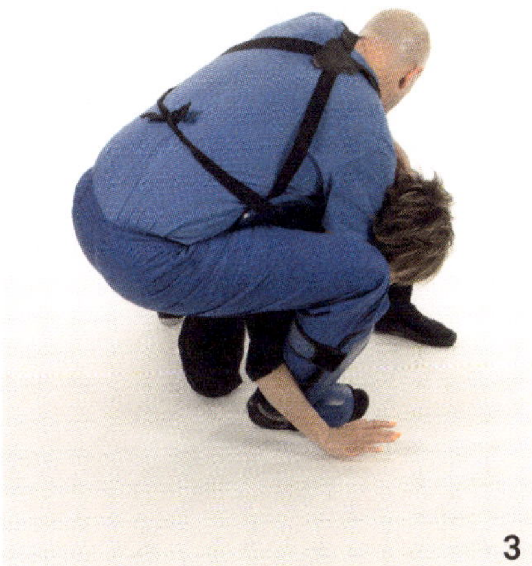

3

4

1. If the attacker shifts his foot forward to stop your action…
2. …reach out and capture his leading leg.
3. Pull his ankle forward towards you and lift.
4. Ram your shoulder into his leg to knock him to the ground, moving your left leg backward to keep him from holding on to you as he falls.

1. If the attacker is much larger than you, you may not be able to pull him down.
2. Kick your legs up and out as far as you can to pull him off balance.
3. Drop to your knees and pull him further forward off balance.
4. Crouch low to propel him forward...
5. ...on to his back.

1

2

3

4

5

Defense against "Full Nelson" Rear Shoulder Lock

1. Adversary reaches his arms up from beneath your arms.
2. Drop your elbows to trap his arms and flex your knees to stabilize yourself.

1

2

3

4

3. Cover his hands with yours, pull down on his arms to lock him in, and head butt him.
4. Peel his hands off and lift his arms up and off your neck.

5. Back under his uplifted arms.
6. Twist his rigid arms into each other.

5

6

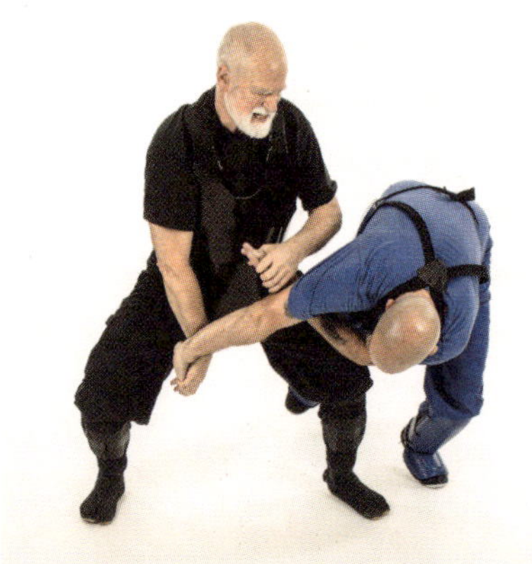

7

8

7. Throw him forward...
8. ...on to his back.
9. If he secures his hands across the back of your neck...
10. ...shift to the side of his topmost hand and pull it off with a rubbing motion.
11. If he grabs with his left hand on top...
12. ...shift to the left and pull his hand off.

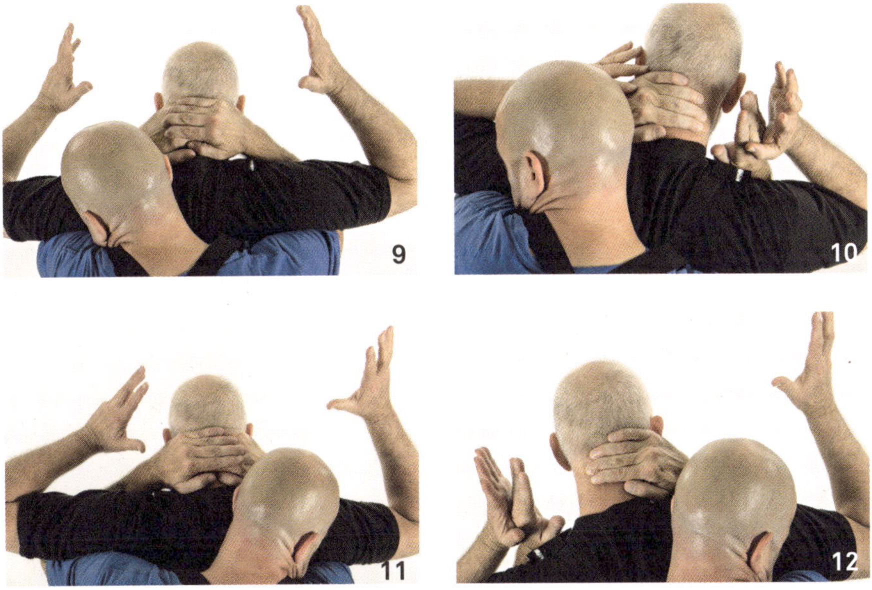

Wind Evasive Escape From Grab Of Lowered Cross Side Hand

1. Aggressor cross grabs your wrist from above (your palm faces down).
2. Turn your hands palm-up and project forward, causing his arm to rotate.

3. Step behind his arm while you pull his arm forward across your mid-section.
4. Pull his arm across your front as you send several elbows back against the side of his head.

Wind Evasive Escape From Grab Of Lowered Mirror Side Hand

1. Aggressor mirror side grabs your wrist from above (your upraised palm faces out).
2. Step around and lay your elbow over his forearm.
3. Pull your trapped hand back and lever down with your elbow.
4. Rock back into him while leveraging his elbow straight.

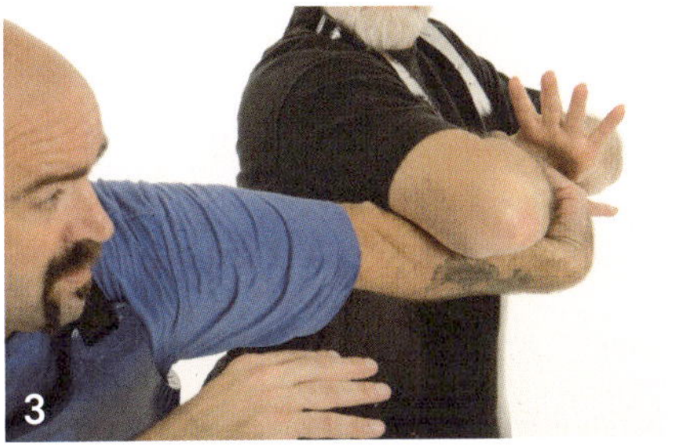

Wind Evasive Escape From Grab Of Raised Cross Side Hand

1. Aggressor cross grabs your wrist from above (your upraised palm faces out).
2. Lift your elbow up and lower your hand behind his forearm...

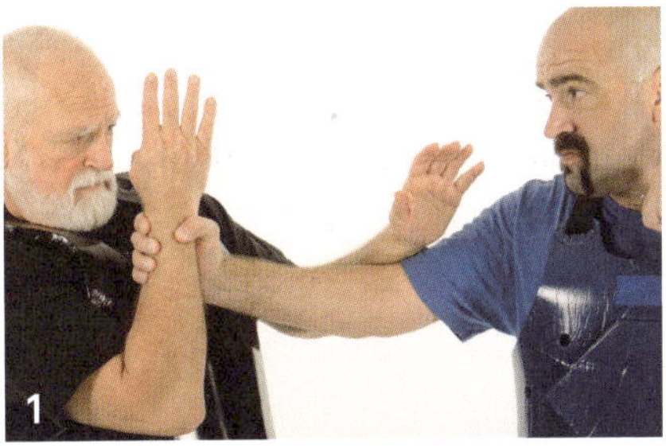

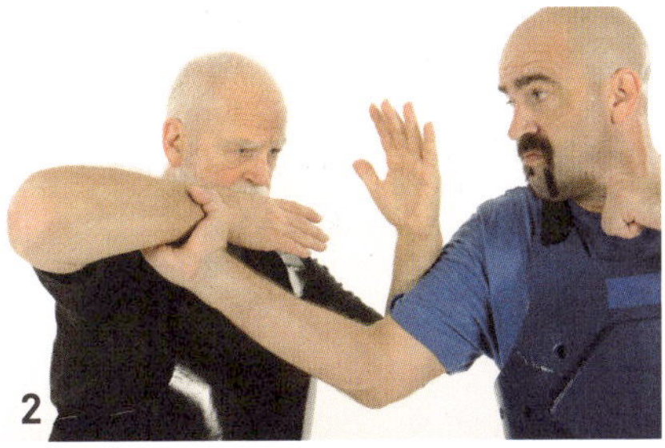

3. ...freeing your hand.
4. Pull back and hook his extended arm against your chest.
5. Slam forward with an elbow to the side oh his head.

Defense Against Choking Attack From Position on Back and on the Ground

1. Adversary straddles you and chokes you with both hands.
2. Reach over with your foot to trap the foot of his kneeling leg.
3. "Buck up" with your hips and shove left with your right palm on his straightened left elbow.

1

2

3

4

5

4. Roll right to throw him forwards on his left shoulder. You can follow with a left knee strike.
5. Suddenly reverse your roll and escape to safety.

Defense against Waist-Tackle Grab; Knee Head, Second Knee, Arm Lever

1. Aggressor crouches …
2. …and rushes in to lift your hand…

3. …and grabs at your leg or waist.
4. Leap back to the side and hit down with a left hand edge strike.
5. Lift your front knee sharply to his head.
6. Pull his head in tightly.
7. Reach out and pull his arm up with an *oh-gyaku* arm bar lift.
8. Step back to pull the attacker forward to the ground.

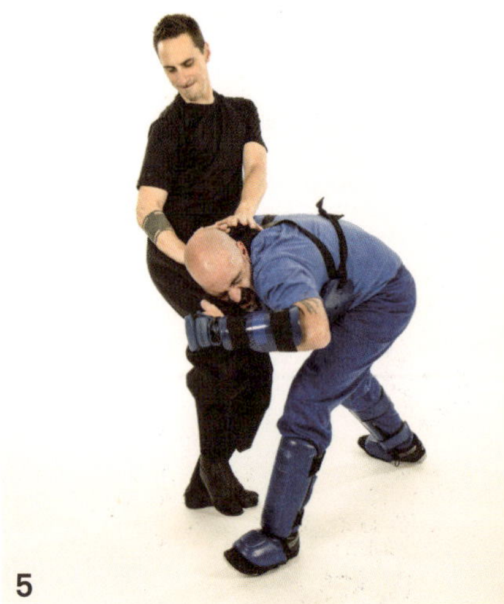

5

6

7

8

Inward Swinging Round Kick with Shin or Toe of Shoe

1. His rear foot swings around...
2. ...and inward with toes.
3. Slip forward inside roundhouse kick with an elbow to the face or chest.
4. Move further in and pick up your leading leg...
5. ...and sweep it back to take out his support leg.
6. Hug and pull up on the leg as he falls on his back.

1

2

3

4

5

6

CHAPTER 7

Void Creativity Realm—
"You Don't See Me. I'm Not Here."

Beyond grounded "earth-strong" stability and command, "water power" secret knowledge,"fire intensity" direct connection, and "wind free" evasiveness, you now explore a fifth elemental possibility—the Ku no Kata "creative source element of the void." In the metaphysics of the ancient Asian traditions, the void is known as the base of all elements. It is a primordial source for all forms that is yet to be set in any form.

The term "void" is an awkward translation from Asian history. The Sanskrit *shunyata* and the Japanese *ku* both mean "emptiness." This sense of being empty implies being unfixed or unrestricted. It means to be empty of any set quality that could exist in and of itself. Everything we could imagine is influenced by countless other factors. Nothing stands alone, uninfluenced by any other influences. This void influence is associated with potential, freedom, creativity, and limitlessness. In human nature, the void manifests as the space-giving personality, and relates to observing far reaching horizons of knowledge, philosophy, or spirituality.

Theme—Confused Ignorance Leads to Broad Ranging Wisdom

The primary void motivation is creative access to higher thinking, acting, and responding. We leave behind conventional thought and behavior, having transcended that. We all want to feel that life is fulfilling and filled with meaning.. We all want to be content with ourselves. We all want to experience directly the significance of life. The void can be described as the motivation to reach the heights of one's personal abilities and talents. In Maslow's words, "What a man can be, he must be."

Under the influence of the void element, we are more independent, creative, constructive, unrestrained, and free. People characterized by the void element prize expressive speech, intellectual freedom, original creativity, and the right to self-determination. Their lives are described as committed, self-directed, and meaningful.

Positive Void "Visionary"

The positive void influence produces a person who is a "master of life" character. He or she is absolutely present, and always finds fulfillment in even the most mundane of situations. The void element could also be seen as inspiring creative multi-talented characters. Void people are able to draw fully upon their potential, as they understand both their strengths and weaknesses and have the self-confidence to determine the best way to employ both. They are seen by others as having good intentions, trustworthy, and expert at what they do. These people are more likely to experience what Maslow describes as "peak experiences" and exist on a higher intellectual plateau than most people.

Positive void sometimes produces what is referred to as "genius". This positive orientation towards space becomes a form of wisdom in which enlightened vision just naturally allows everything to advance towards achieving illumination. This approach is perfectly content to allow the grander scheme of totality to bring about the fruition of that which must be. ***Creative, self-fulfilling, unpredictable***, and ***unique*** would be words typically used by others in describing a "positive void" person.

Negative Void "Space case" and "Guru trip"

Under the *weak* void influence, a person is "spaced out" due to a lack of personal commitment or discipline. Anything is acceptable. All is accepted as reasonable. These people tend to be past or future or "other" oriented, and can have problems relating to the here and now. They think of themselves as creative, but do not produce anything but self-serving criticism of what is popularly accepted around them. This type was particularly prevalent as a life style orientation in the hippie age of the late 1960s.

Strong negative void manifests as the eccentric "guru figure," smug and self satisfied, seeking converts to serve as supports for his or her ego. This type is often self-indulgent in an irresponsible manner. Anything is

OK, as long as things go along smoothly. Murder-suicide groups including Charles Manson's "family" and Jim Jones' People's Temple in the 1970s, Rajneesh's Oregon commune in the 1980s, and the Japanese Om Shinri Kyo cult in the 1990s, remind us of the eerie power of the negative void in effect.

As a limitation, the void personality can easily get caught up in the vastness of indecision and distracted activity, even at cost of losing something that could easily have been created for the benefit of all with little effort. We can become so involved in seeing the grand picture and allowing everyone their space that we cease to be effective as an agent of progress. ***Deluded, dreamer, "spacey,"*** and ***erratic*** would be words typically used by others in describing a "negative void" type.

Negative Expression	Positive Expression
Eccentric	Marches to a different drummer
Ungrounded	Creative
Undisciplined	Free
Day-dreamy	Sense of fascination
Idle	Peaceful

The mandala symbol for the void element is the *dharma-chakra*, or "wheel of highest universal laws". In ancient days in Asia, only royalty or the highest aristocracy was permitted to travel with wheeled vehicles. With eight spokes reaching out in all directions, the wheel symbolizes the ideal of the vehicle that can deliver insight in whichever direction and whatever form is required. The essence of infinite space and timelessness, the void influence is further symbolized by the color bright white and is placed in the center of the mandala in relation to the other elements.

How This Shows Up in Unarmed Combat

Have you gained the skill of *sensing the aggressor's intention* and going with the logical technique instead of focusing on what you are prepared to do? The greater lesson is how to give the aggressor the impression that he is winning, and then surprisingly defeating him.

Some people mistake this for "unfocused uncertainty." This is not at all an accurate interpretation. You are actually letting go of a preconceived idea of what is happening in order to generate best advantage. A parallel would be fighting a ghost. Would you try to grasp a ghost with your hands, or would you use its insubstantiality to trick it into submission? Would you be better off ignoring the ghost and moving confidently about your space?

Have you gained the skill of *doing the unexpected when a more conventional response might be the norm?* You set him up for confusion when he expects conventional resistance from you? The greater lesson is how to take best advantage of what is coming your way in such a manner as to thoroughly confuse the attacker.

Have you gained the skill of *changing the element that your aggressor is trying to angle you into responding from*? The greater lesson is how to jump from element to element in order to make yourself unconquerable.

There are no set forms or *kata* to illustrate the void element in To-Shin Do. We practice how to move effortlessly from one element to another in order to be hard to understand or predict. We lead the aggressor one way and then at the point of delivery we suddenly go another way. Relying on a standard admonition of "back straight, knees bent, hands up," which guides us through all the elements, we nonetheless are free to adapt and interpret in order to be unpredictable.

We can also use creative or counterintuitive verbal or postural responses to throw off an attacker. By answering probing or hostile questions with illogical or confusing words, we can buy a few moments to be better prepared for what we are pressured to deal with. The attacker cannot figure us out.

PART 3

Applications

CHAPTER 8

Sounds of the Elements

In ancient days on Japanese battlefields, little attention was paid to verbalization during conflict. Probably a fiercely growled "Aargh!" routinely accompanied stabs with a spear or cleaving swings with a sword.

The image of the ninja defeating an anonymous villain carries the legend onward.

Today, when street attacks are so up-close and personal, laws permit dangerous people to get very close to you before they launch an assault.

It is more than likely that a verbal attack, or at least a verbal probe, will happen before he moves on you. For this reason, it is imperative that we explore the role of the voice in the playing out of confrontations.

I think it is reasonable to say sound can intensify or even change one's state. Think of soothing a beleaguered friend with a breathy "There, there, there..." The sound projects your wish externally. Then think of breathing out a deep "Ahhh..." when sinking into a huge cushy chair at the end of a frantic day. That sound receives your wish internally.

Tone and place in the body from which the sound emerges can vary with differing results. Think of a high tight projected cat scream, like Bruce Lee used so famously in his movies. It comes "from the heart." Now think of a low ragged rumbling growl of determination, a do-or-die eruption. That comes "from the gut." Can you imagine the type of movement that would honestly emerge from each?

The word itself used does not seem to have anything to do with logic or literal meaning. When you are confident of yourself in a fight, you might evade skillfully and counter with a breathy "Easy, easy, my friend." from high in your lungs with a neutral face. The same "Easy, easy..." from high in the lungs but with a piercing quality and an evil smile will have a very different effect on the adversary. One soothes. One eggs on frustratingly, in fact encouraging the exact opposite of taking it easy.

Here is a curiosity. Why aren't personal, individual, specific triggering verbal assaults more addressed in martial arts training? Such use of words seems to be integral to most social aggression. Verbal insults and threats are designed to increase the defenders sense of invasion and resulting confusion as survival considerations are weighed. Yes, but simple physical fight training seems to be the focus of most instructors though. Techniques start with the situation after the fight has begun. What is so lacking would seem to be an important part. Yet most martial arts instructors just leave the verbalization out.

What is happening in those seconds of verbal assault that could lead up to a physical assault? How best to strategically respond, understanding that the aggressor is just blindly pushing buttons, hoping that one will have an effect on you? How do you elevate your brain, to see how you might de-escalate the situation? How do you keep from being hijacked by a knee-jerk lower brain response of spontaneously unplanned physical action?

In any kind of conflict or confrontation, the voice is reflected by the choice of element. Are you taking charge of the situation? Are you responding to changing circumstances? Are you moving to confuse him? Are you looking to evade and avoid engagement?

Start with a deep abdominal sound of AH. This is the sound your body makes when you are totally relaxed. Imagine collapsing into a lounge chair at the end of a busy day. *Ahhhh*. Also imagine you are in a commanding state. For the earth element, make a deep AH sound from deep in your body, as in the command to "stop." Say this word with a guttural growl as "Staahp" or "Cut it out." Say this with your body totally relaxed and your mouth fully open.

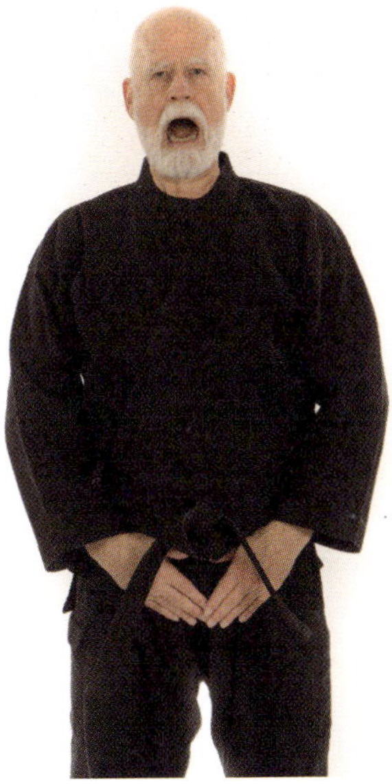

AH is the base verbalization.

OH is the gut-level verbalization.

Next, say an OH sound. Imagine what you would utter upon making a breakthrough discovery. *Ohhhh!* This sound comes from your gut, with just a little tension to it. Responding to an aggressor's movement, you reply with a "no" or "don't." Coming from the water element, where you tactically reposition to win, tighten your abdomen and say this word with a gutsy rasp as *"Noh"* or *"Whoa" or Oh no you don't."* Say this while adding a little tension to your face, to where your mouth forms an "oh" shape.

Third in the sequence is the vowel EH sound. This comes from your solar plexus, with even more body tension. Imagine what you would say when you discover a sneak thief trying to inch over to your purse or briefcase. *HeyHeyHey!* Interrupting an aggressor as he prepares to move against you, you bark out a sharp "Hey" or "Get back!" command from the fire element. Pop the sound out from your midsection as an interjected *"Hey! Get back!"* Speak this from a tenser face, where your teeth almost touch and your lips are pulled to the sides.

EH is the solar plexus verbalization.

II is the heart-level verbalization.

Fourth is an II ("eeee") vowel sound from your heart. Imagine trying to soothe a spooked horse with a gentle *Easy, easy...* Feel the sound come from the center of your chest, between your arms. This comes from the wind element in a calm upper register "Easy." Breathe out the sound as you move to evade his technique from the wind element as *"Eeasy..."* or *"Peace."* This is said with your teeth together and your lips pulled to the sides.

UU is the throat verbalization.

Finally, as a fifth elemental void or ether sound, you make a light UU ("ouuu") sound. This comes from your throat, with a light unaffected nature as "Suit yourself…." Practice this as *"Suuit yourself…"* and move to where you confuse him or take away his attack advantage. Say this sound with your lips barely parted.

AH, OH, EI, II, UU can be practiced as elemental vocals along with your fighting response from any of the five elemental reactions. From the earth, command him to "stahp." From the water, react to his trick with *"oh no you don't."* From fire, cut him short with *"hey!"* From the wind element, slip past his damage with *"eeasy…"* If you are practicing a creative or confusing response from the void element, baffle him with a *"suit yourself…."*

AH OH EI II UU finally end up with teeth and lips pressed fully together for an MMNN sound. This will give you the classic A-U-M or OM mantra. In the Japanese alphabet, the first sound is AH and the final sound is that MMNN. You are completing the entire Japanese alphabet with your A-U-M.

The five sounds are a way to coordinate your actions with your words. It is also true that if you are making noise, you will necessarily be breathing out. This is opposed to sucking in a breath and holding it in fear. Get used to projecting the words in a loud and distracting manner as you practice your techniques.

As a further practice, you can try saying short sentences that interrupt a bully or aggressor before he actually moves to physical action. Here are some suggestions for handling a verbal bully. He is using words to demean you, making fun of your appearance, your body, what you are striving for, or how you are dressed. He has not taken physical action against you yet, but you suspect it is imminent. Be aware of the five elements and where the words come from in your body. Low guttural command? Tightened solar plexus interjection? From the heart utterance?

From the earth center of command, you interrupt a bully's put down remarks from the base of your torso, "OK. I've had enough. I'm leaving." Say it as an abrupt command with a firm deep voice. Stare into his eyes as you say it, turn, and no matter what he says next, walk away, checking out of the corner of your eye to be sure he does not move against you from behind.

From a water approach, you tighten your stomach and move the bullying to an unexpected place. Express yourself slowly and make it sound sincere (even if it is not necessarily sincere). "I used to look up to you. I thought you were so cool. Why are you doing this now?" Back away shaking your head no, and when at a safe distance, turn and move away from him quickly.

From the fire center of forward action and initiative, you raise your hands palm-out to interrupt the bully's chatter and say, "You just lost the best friend you could have ever had." As the bully responds, wave your hands in dismissal. Turn abruptly and walk away, again checking out of the corner of your eye to monitor a possible advance from him.

From a wind approach of evasion and slipping away, brush one hand back and forth in front of you as if you were fanning away smoke and say very slowly, "I… just don't have time for this." Do not look at his eyes. Move to the side, give him lots of room, and walk off. Do not respond to anything that he shouts after you.

With the above elemental response suggestions, it is important to practice the responses many times before you need them. You could even try saying them in the mirror to check out how you look when verbalizing them. You need to appear to speak spontaneously, but it will take lots of practice to override your natural brain freeze-up when confronted. You have to practice over and over again to look spontaneous.

An aggressor may try to "interview" you to see if you are somebody he wants to engage. He might ask you impossible-to-answer questions to get you into your head groping for an answer. While you are distracted, trying to reason with him in his unreasonableness, he attacks. "What are you looking at?" could be his probe. "I'm just admiring that jacket you're wearing," you could reply in a diffusing comment. "You staring at my girl?" he might throw out. You could reply, "Ah, caught me. You must be so happy, my friend." He might confront you with, "You got a problem?" You act like you do not get the confrontation and say, "Yeah. I was supposed to meet my wife fifteen minutes ago. She's not here. That's not like her."

Things could be at a more advanced stage and someone or a group of people have threatened you and challenged you to a fight. Keep your distance and keep your face relaxed. Keep your shoulders relaxed, elbows low, and hands raised casually but strategically. Say what you have to say to get yourself out of there.

"You're the third person today who wants to kick my butt. I'm making everybody mad at me. Hey, I apologize. Why don't you get in your truck and I'll get in mine and we'll go our separate ways?"

"No. No. You're looking for my brother-in-law. He's a real jerk. No doubt he's the one who made you mad. Hey, whip him for me too. I'm gonna just take off now."

"I'm just looking to watch the ball game and have some friendly conversation. Looks like this isn't the place. I'm out of here."

"Oh man. You're way too tough for me. I'm just going to take my tired rear end and get out of here and leave you alone. Have a great day now."

Speak the lines from a relaxed state. Breathe in and out of your nose, not your mouth. Breathing through your nose has a distinct effect on your brain chemistry, different from pulling in air through your opened mouth. Speak from your gut, and try to talk slowly. This is quite different from speaking hurriedly and from high in your chest. That is a sure tip-off that you are frightened or confused.

Be careful of your word choice. Again, it must be stressed that this takes practice, just like your fighting skills. Rehearse these lines, or something else specifically created by you for you for situations you are likely to find yourself in. Be careful how you express yourself spontaneously. "I don't want to fight" with upraised hands plays right into an aggressor's intentions. He knows that; that is exactly why he has selected you. He doesn't want to fight either. He wants to administer a beating. Instead, confuse him with, "No need for violence here" from the gut. Likewise, a statement of "I don't want any trouble," is likely to be met with, "Yeah? Well you got trouble." Instead, say, "Nothing needs to happen here."

Also be very careful to avoid language that can get you into difficulty with law enforcement. What are witnesses hearing as you go back-and-forth with a yapping aggressor before it comes to physical action? In heat-of-the-moment response to an uncalled-for attack, you can get yourself in trouble. "I'm gonna kick your butt!" or "Yeah? Well bring it on!" or "Let's do this!" show a willingness to engage in a fight, which is not what you want to have come up in a courtroom where you are being tried. What do witnesses hear? Words like "Stop" or "No, don't" or Hey" or "Easy" will work much more favorably in your defense.

Post fight, when the police show up, you too are likely to be taken in while police figure out what happened. Be very careful what you say. Police are trained to be tricky. In trying to figure out who did what to whom, they may ask you, "Were you scared?" Avoid by all means tough guy answers like, "No, I wasn't scared. He just had no right to talk to me like that." or "He made a disrespectful kissy noise at my wife." Definitely the wrong answers. Tell the authorities, "I was very scared. I feared for my life. I felt he intended to do severe damage to me. I felt that he possessed the capability to do severe damage to me. I could find no way out; he cornered me and left me no choice but to physically defend myself."

Practice this until it becomes your habit. Focus on the three points: He intended to do me harm. He had the capability of doing me harm. As he approached I could find no escape. When apprehended, just repeat that over and over, until you are represented by an attorney.

In today's world the criminals and bullies often get away with their antisocial actions, and are even rewarded by schools and the courts. You need to do everything possible to bend the odds in your favor. This means adding carefully planned verbal interactions to your physical training regimen. Then practice those responses as often as you practice your physical techniques.

CHAPTER 9

How Do We Handle Bullying?

Bullying seems to be on the unfortunate rise these days. Or at least it now gets more of our attention. In schools and workplaces, people routinely find pleasure in making others unhappy. Individuals in positions of power prey on those perceived as lacking power, make them feel bad, and derive joy from it. This has created quite a problem for school administrators. Bullying happens. When school administrators attempt to resolve the problem, the bully's parents (who as bullies themselves taught the child to bully) attack the school with complaints and law suits. This causes the schools to hesitate to confront bullies, in order to avoid difficulty. And so the problem continues uninterrupted.

This also is a problem in the workplace. Bullying or harassment happens. The bullied worker hesitates to report it, for (rightful?) fear of being retaliated against by a superior. Corporate management positions to avoid bad publicity or a lawsuit, and it is written off as the word of one employee against another. This lack of wanting to get involved on the part of corporations continues unabated, and a culture of cruelty or reduced expectations develops within.

Where does this bullying come from? Why do some people feel happy only when they cause others to suffer? Why do some human beings seem to delight in bringing others pain and distress? What causes some to want to go out of their way to make life miserable for others? Where does this urge to demean and degrade begin?

We might expect hostile behavior from mentally ill persons, social misfits, or persons deprived of the basic needs of life. Such individuals might choose violence towards others from a sense of having nothing left to lose. "If I'm miserable and unlucky and ugly, why should anyone else get to be happy and gifted and beautiful?" the illogic might read. Such violent treatment of others is not normal healthy behavior. So why would otherwise stable, healthy, and productive people choose to foster sadness in others' lives? Why would someone with plenty of constructive resources want to spend their energies working for others' downfall?

The Nature of the Beast

We might look to the traditional wisdom of Asia, to the structure of the body and its personality for the answers. According to the ancient mind sciences that have been a part of Japan's spiritual legacy since the early sixth century, there may be a part of our human nature that needs to be a defender of territory. It *demands to be exercised*. We follow the urge to compete with others for scarce resources. We pit ourselves against others to determine dominance in a world where the dominant get what they need, and all others suffer lack.

Each of us comes pre-programmed, hard-wired with this protector nature as a part of our make-up. This warrior or defender aspect is only one of many character-shaping forces of course. The famous Swiss psychologist Carl G. Jung, intrigued with Asian spiritual disciplines, referred to these universal inner forces as "archetypes." As a working part of the total self, this defender urge seeks to be expressed. It wants to make its contribution. It experiences a need to fulfill the duty of protecting the self from hostile advances of whatever would destroy the self. It seeks its reward in the preservation of order and the enjoyment of victory.

In ancient times, this defender or competitor archetype was a critically important aspect. In those centuries before the establishment of courts, policing forces, and laws, the warrior or defender aspect was crucial for survival. Only the strong prevailed. Such a warrior response was the only thing that stood as a barrier to savage brutalization.

Too often in modern society, however, this warrior defender part of the personality lacks opportunity to exercise itself. For the majority of persons, life is so safe. It is utterly devoid of any real need for a personal defender archetype. In most civilized societies, there are few cases of clear-cut aggression against which we must use defensive capability. Few of us ever have to fight for our lives. No true enemy ever appears to face against us. Therefore, the defender archetype does not get the chance to feel needed. It rarely has the opportunity to earn its keep. But that competitive part of the self still needs an enemy to justify its own existence.

So much so that without an invader to provide a challenge to meet, we will create the illusion of an enemy to be resisted and confronted. The defender within will create a threat without in order to be needed.

Sometimes our urges to encounter the thrill of the need to defend take simple guises. We invest hours watching pro ball teams - our own (the "good") and the other (the "bad"). When those players we support win, we take to the streets with drunken shrieks of "We're number one!" and we cheerfully lord our victory over the gloomy fans of the defeated team.

However, sometimes our need to exercise our inner defender character takes on a more ominous form. We strive for the experience of significance in our quick willingness to find foes in the world. We cast about and identify some group of people to whom we can assign the role of enemy. Once the assignment is made, we are committed. Whether along economic, racial, geographical, political, religious, or cultural dividing lines, we can conveniently direct our defensive wrath at those who are not like us.

We have to exercise our defender nature. This need is a part of our human genetic inheritance. Some inner part of the self hungers for the cold excitement of being part of a grand struggle against dark powers. We need to feel that we are important enough to be targeted. We need to think of ourselves as being consequential enough to warrant being taken seriously. Therefore, in our demand for the direct experience of our own significance, we search for a dragon against which we can throw our warrior energies. We get to strive gallantly to overcome an enemy.

Grander Competition against Greater Foes

In a view characteristic of the Buddhist mind sciences developed in the Himalayan foothills over two thousand years ago, competition for survival between groups can be seen as the *middle* level of three competitive possibilities. There is a degraded form of the defender urge, a middle ground, and an enlightened version of the drive. Competition between groups and between members of the same group has always been a part of the human experience. This competitive struggle focuses on dealing with *negative effects perceived as stemming from hostile others*. We conquer the others, and life returns to normal.

However, if everyone concentrated on getting the best for themselves, the world would be an acceptable place. You strive for upliftment and I strive for upliftment, and we both get the best we can. We compete with conditions. We defend against happenings that would bring everybody down. We strive along side each other to beat those things that would overpower us, and we both win. That is the middle ground of our competitive nature. Below the middle is a territory lower than the conventional archetypal acting out of defender nature. Competition within the group, at cost to the group's grander welfare, is seen as a *degradation* of the competitive defender urge. This lower level competition is the defender archetype in a demeaned or smaller form. We fight those we know we can beat.

This small competitive nature creates a need to bully in order to feel dominant. "If I do not bully, I will be bullied," is the illogic. The innate urge to defend against invasion can degenerate into simple mean-spirited joy over the reduction of other people's lives. We cast about for a less than threatening opponent and move against him. Our ability to bully another is our assurance that we are indeed dominant. We are important. We matter. We win.

But what would the natural inclination toward exercising our warrior protector nature look like if ennobled through an enlightened perspective? If it is possible to degrade the urge for the stimulation of competition, it must therefore be possible to do the opposite, to uplift the urge. What if we took it to an "above the middle" position? You escape the primitive "got to crush them before they crush me" mentality. Is it possible to reach the third state and elevate the focus of your personality's inner need to exercise the warrior defender? You become a protector. You defend others against predators.

In feudal Japan, the *samurai* warrior aristocrats were given the responsibility for keeping the peace, enforcing the laws, and governing the land. Born into their elite social class, they were the only ones permitted to carry swords. Up until the late 1860s, these samurai were in effect a roving combination of police, jury, judge, and executioner all rolled into one. They had the duty to kill to uphold the law if necessary. They used discretion, historical precedent, and dispassionate fairness to avoid the temptation to abuse their powers.

Historically, Japan's noble *samurai* warriors were pledged to a very specific hierarchy of allegiances. Serving as many people as possible with a single commitment was the highest ideal. First and foremost, the aristocratic warrior willingly pledged to defend his or her territory. Second on the list was loyalty to the community. This was the specific area in which he or she lived. Further down on the list was devotion to immediate family. In last place was concern for oneself. In focusing on the broadest possible level of serving others, the ancient warrior served him or herself in the most effective way conceivable.

Such a selfless commitment to protecting others might sound impossible for us in the American land of rugged individualism (at least in our cultural myths we are rugged individualists). Some might scoff at such a noble commitment as too idealistic. "Good luck with that working in the real world," the jaded might smirk in derision.

But the truth of the grander ideal of the compassionate warrior is still as valid today. Focus on improving the broader picture, and you win in the most magnificent way. By improving the condition of the natural environment, you have a purer and healthier world in which to live. By improving the lives of others in your community, you are surrounded by happier and more helpful people. Allow yourself to see the bigger picture and you automatically enlarge your personal experience of life. This view of competition only sounds strange or corny because such grander commitments to one's fellow human beings seem so rare these days. It is much more common to fall into the cynicism, greed, and tight vision born of fear. "Everyone else has sold out," we rationalize. "Why should I be the only ethical one left?"

Perhaps it could be argued that we have earned the right to our cynicism. Too many of our heroes turned out to be corruptible. A parade of tainted pretenders somehow slithered up onto the pedestals we built for heroes. We recoiled when we saw our nation's top elected officials, religious ministers, celebrities, and sports idols toppled one after another by headlines of disappointing behavior and outright betrayal. We remember clearly the sting of being let down. We naively believed that those we called heroes would act heroically, simply because we thought of them as heroes. We felt disgust and anger for having been tricked into believing in them.

But then, could not our disillusionment be transformed into a new call for a revival of the potential grandness of everybody? We need to raise our sights and see the greater enemy that looms behind the smaller distractions. If the force of the warrior defender archetype is part of our natural human constitution, should we not engage that force to defeat a truly noble adversary, some ultimate enemy truly worthy of us? Perhaps it is once again right to embrace the noble ideals of the enlightened warrior protector who campaigns to uplift all of humanity.

Bullies bully because it feels good to have power over someone else. That is the degraded sense of the warrior defender being exercised. What if we reversed that? What if we experienced the power to make someone's day? What if we exercised the defender archetype in a positive elevated manner? How would it feel to campaign to make another person a little brighter, a little more positive about the daily grind? What would that person think of you? How would they regard you?

Have you ever caused someone to smile? A person was going about their day distracted and frazzled and you said something that so cheered them up that they stopped and smiled at you. Have you ever made someone's day? They were stumbling along and you said or did just the right thing that illuminated their whole day and brought them a little brightness. Have you ever saved anyone? Someone was going down, and you put yourself aside and took a risk and reached out and grabbed them. Which feels better? Which makes you feel more powerful? Tearing people down, or building people up?

Opposite of a bully who gets his kicks out of making others miserable, how might it feel to be a rescuer, a person who brings others up? A savior? How would it feel to be a bringer of joy? How would it feel to be looked up to as someone powerful enough to make the day brighter?

Vow to become the opposite of a bully. Fill the role of a protector, not a predator. You will exercise your defender nature by building up other people, not singling them out for pain. You have studied the skills of personal protection, so you have less to fear. You are bigger than the small dark hearts that live out their defender nature in ways that abuse. You channel your defender nature towards finding and elevating those who are oppressed. You become the ultimate winner, surrounded by others who get to win too.

CHAPTER 10

A Guide for Advancement

In To-Shin Do study, the physical techniques and strategic handling of conflict are joined by a third area of endeavor - a guide for self-advancement. Through the three-fold study of physical tactics, strategic handling of the street or field, and philosophical consideration, you are changing as a human being. To change is to grow. When you have changed very much, it will mean that you have grown very much.

We begin with a three-part promise to ourselves to fully commit to the three parts of any self-advancement program. We believe we can do it. We believe in what we are aiming at. We believe in those who are mentoring us.

Seeker's Creed

What you need more than anything else in the beginning of your To-Shin Do self empowerment program is a firm foundation as to what you expect of yourself. From there you can build up the momentum you need to succeed in accomplishing any goal in life.

Experience shows that the common enemies of the spirit encountered by all of us at various times in life are:

- **False ideals** ... that breed lack of self-confidence and will to win
- **False creeds**... that breed confusion or lead us in the wrong direction
- **False friends**... that breed smallness, cynicism, and doubt

What we need more than anything else in the beginning are

- **Noble ideals**
- **Workable plans**
- **True allies**

Promise yourself that you will make a commitment to awakening the potential for living life fully. Your promise taps into the potential inherent in the three treasures of:

- ***Ji-shin* confidence...for noble ideals**
  a whole new concept of what you can become
- ***Tan-ren* discipline...for workable plans**
  a whole new range of what you can learn and master
- ***Son-kei* respect...for worthy allies**
  a whole new community of friends and teachers

I believe in myself.
I am confident.
I can accomplish my goals.

If you do not believe you can do it, you are defeated before you even begin. Start with a pledge to activate the highest potential within you. See your own future development reflected in the skills and knowledge of those who began before you.

Have you ever known someone who did not believe in himself or herself? Watching them, perhaps even trying to encourage them on and then encountering their resistance, you learned that motivation can only come from within.

I believe in what I study.
I am disciplined.
I am ready to learn and advance.

If you do not believe in what you are working to develop, what is the point of study? Look and examine and compare, and come to a firm belief in the program you have engaged in.

When you are inspired by the ideal of knowing more about what is *really true* about life, you are just naturally drawn towards that which will encourage growth. Even at the expense of letting go of old and familiar cherished limitations, you can not help but be motivated to explore on.

I believe in my teachers.
I show respect for all who help me progress.

Even the greatest of all champions have coaches and trainers they can rely on to bring out the best in them. A good teacher is a treasure in your life. Think of all the people who have helped you by providing encouragement, advice, support, and a living example of how to get what you know you deserve.

A truly powerful person is comfortable acknowledging the accomplishments and worthiness of others. Extend respect to get respect. To salute and repay all those who cared enough to help you grow, be a great practitioner and encourage others in turn.

Mindful Action Code

There are fourteen specific bad habits that account for most of the self-induced misery in the world. One or more of these fourteen are part of all crimes committed and punished, loving relationships disrupted and broken, jobs failed, friendships ruined, and nations going to war against each other. Stretching across all times and cultures, these fourteen weaknesses are so easy to slip into despite their inability to generate positive results.

Use this code of mindful action to avoid having to make important life-quality decisions under pressure. Prepare now. Question each of the 14 points as to its truth! Make every day a practice of transcending unconscious "auto-pilot" or "sleep-walk" living. Wake up!

I protect life and health.
I avoid violence whenever possible.

Develop your ability to serve as a protector. Wherever you go, everyone is a little safer and more secure because you are there. The world already has too many predators. Retaliating with even more cruelty will not solve our problems. Whenever possible, be bigger than the pull of petty vengeance and violence. Make the world a safer place for all.

I respect the property and space of all.
I avoid taking what has not been offered.

Stealing things, money, resources, ideas, loyalties, and credit for accomplishment eats away at your own sense of personal worth. Do not degenerate to the level of a lowly parasite, stealing the efforts of others who work to produce value in the world. Look around for what you can do to be of such value to others that you thereby generate legitimately all that you need.

I develop significant relationships.
I avoid abusing others for selfish gain.

Do not treat others' hearts in a reckless way. Encourage significance, empowerment, and trust through authentic friendship. Users, abusers, seducers, rapists, and con artists, demean the beauty of what they twist into use for their own pleasure. Model your relationships on the way you would want others to treat your parents or your children.

I thoughtfully express the truth.
I avoid the confusion of dishonest words.

Be real. No one respects a phony. No one wants to invest time in a fake. Lying to self and others makes it impossible to live with integrity, and you will not impress people for long. Liars are annoying and pathetic at the least and destructive and damaging at the most. Be sure that your words match your actions, and your actions match your words.

I cultivate a positive attitude, a healthy body, and a clear mind.
I avoid whatever would reduce my physical or mental well-being.

Do not mistreat yourself. It is easy to get hooked on destructive and addictive distractions that lead away from clear consciousness. Alcohol, nicotine, drugs, and even food or affection or the internet can lure us into a false illusion of contentment with life. Avoid escapes from clarity. Enjoy the vibrant health that results from facing life square on.

I communicate health, happiness, and peace of mind to everyone I meet.
I avoid violent, disturbing, and unduly critical speech.

To compete with the savage noisy clamor that dominates so many lives, you can be tempted to match the sheer volume and harshness with your own voice. Severe criticism of others can suggest fear and insecurity on the part of the critic. Bold talk without real action is cheap. Use assuring and encouraging words to reconcile and resolve any conflicts, and build up your friends.

I promote harmony and positive momentum to bring out the best in everyone.
I avoid causing alienation, doubt, and division among others.

No one respects a troublemaker, back-stabber, or two-faced two-timer. Putting down others to build yourself up just adds more negative energy to an already fractured world. Work to build a reputation of being one who encourages positive momentum in other people's lives. Be the winner.

I encourage all to speak purposefully from the heart.
I avoid the dull contentment of gossip and small talk.

Avoid the nervous habit of talking on with fluffy chatter to fill in silence or hidie from your true feelings and observations. Do not spread stories that you do not know to be fact. Avoid whisper campaigns that have the sole purpose of hurting others. Speak with grounded words from the heart, or purposefully withhold speech and save your energy if that better expresses the needs of the moment.

I am as enthusiastic about others' fulfillment as I am about my own.
I avoid treating others' successes as the cause of my lacks.

Resenting or envying what others have created undermines your own self-esteem. You do not need that. Do not delude yourself into thinking of others as "lucky" and yourself as not. Rejoice in the good fortune of others. There is one more happy person making up your world. One more person serves as a good example of the positive potential for you and everyone else.

I promote the enjoyment of life, and encourage others with my smile.
I avoid setting myself against the world.

Hostility, anger, and maliciousness are easy habits to develop. See them as the traps they are. Bring ease to your life. Be kind to yourself. Show strength by choosing compassion. Look for ways to improve the quality of others' days, thereby improving your experience of the world you inhabit.

I strive for the personal realization of truth.
I avoid the seductive comfort of narrow-mindedness.

Operating from a set of beliefs or principles that do not match authentic reality makes life confusing and hard to endure. Strive to look beyond your own personal "conventional truth" to realize the grander timeless "ultimate truth" that underpins all of our experiences. Focus more on coming up with new questions than defending old answers.

I accomplish what must be done in a timely and effective way.
I avoid putting off what will benefit me and my world today.

You never get a "day off" from life. Do it now. Enjoy making each precious moment count for something.

I strive to be so strong that nothing can disturb my peace of mind.
I avoid the negative effects of worry, doubt, and regret.

Be cheerful and optimistic. Look for the brightness and value in every encounter and experience. Vow to create a life in which you find yourself too big for worry, too majestic for doubt, too grand for anger, and too strong for fear.

I work to build love, happiness, and loyalty among all members of my family.
I avoid putting temporary personal benefit ahead of the welfare of those I love.

Skillfully express your appreciation and encouragement to each member of your family. Do not let the years together lead you to taking them for granted. No other success can justify failure in the home.

8-Step Accomplishment Plan

After making a promise to succeed, then living up to a code of ethical behavior, To-Shin Do students turn to a plan for inner advancement.. Whenever dreams are turned into reality, a group of eight specific personal qualities are almost always present in the process. Conversely, lack of these eight qualities accounts for the vast majority of failures to create what we need in life.

Learn how to gain control of the process by which you create your future. Promise yourself to observe the eight steps of the accomplishment plan as a method for turning dreams into goals, goals into objectives, objectives into tasks, and tasks into steps to produce what you need.

Ultimate Truth is Ultimate!

I see life as it really is and stay tuned in!
Verify it!

Allow yourself to develop a proper mindset or perspective. That is the most important asset you bring to your personal quest for a fulfilling life. Be ready to change your mind about the way you believe things are. The ultimate secret is that nothing really is the way we think it looks. Seek out everything that can expand your perspective on the true significance of the experience of life. Let all you encounter serve to guide you towards advancing wholeness. Are you ready for that?

I take charge of inner vision and set my mind on what I need to see!
Visualize it!

Simply think a thing and you create its reality. The subconscious mind is programmed through repeated input. With a positive and healthy attitude, your thoughts just naturally guide your speech and actions towards proper constructive progress. Vow to create an inner vision of only that which you wish to experience.

I communicate truth and say what I need to hear!
Verbalize it!
What the subconscious mind encounters over and over again becomes the core of its contents. What you hear often enough becomes the reality

that you experience around you. Speak what you seek.

I work constructively to generate what I need to experience!
Vitalize it!

When the world sees you going about the business of living in a way consistent with your inner vision and expressed intention, then the world presumes that life experience to be your reality. The world figures that if you look like a happy and enlightened being, think like a happy and enlightened being, sound like a happy and enlightened being, deal with others like a happy and enlightened being, then you must be a happy and enlightened being.

I take responsibility for what surrounds me in the world!
Vantage!

Examine all your choices. If your days are filled with negative encounters, it is because somehow you have chosen to live around negative people. If your days are filled with negative events, it is because somehow you have chosen to live in negative surroundings. If your days are filled with negative actions, it is because somehow you have chosen to live with negative occupations. If you do not take responsibility for the influences that shape your life, who will? Make the choice to make a choice.

I keep positive momentum going and make the right things happen!
Valor!

Some are known as dreamers of great dreams. Others awaken and get to work. Courage, enthusiasm, and diligence will be required of those championing the triumph of intelligence, compassion, and wisdom. Get moving!

I use every experience as an opportunity to grow. Everything matters!
Vigilance!

Every moment has its lesson. Stay mindful of all the possibilities. What is the higher value of what you are experiencing right now? What is there to learn and enjoy right here? Each and every encounter experience could provide the final piece of the puzzle that lifts us to enlightened peace of spirit.

Consistent concentration! I center my spirit right here right now!
Veracity!

Take the time to practice paying attention to paying attention. Watch from the inside out in a calm, clear, and scientific manner. Practice being mindful even when you think you do not need to be mindful. Beyond all hopes and habits, who are you? Look at how you appear. Talk about how you speak. Ponder over how you think. Develop the habit of questioning all habits.

An-shu Rumiko and An-shu Stephen thank their "attacker" Mike Messner.

About the Author

"One of the ten most influential living martial artists in the world."
—*Black Belt Magazine*

Stephen K. Hayes has spent his entire adult life in pursuit of perfection through the Asian martial arts and spiritual traditions. He began his training in the martial arts at Miami University in Oxford, Ohio, in 1967. In 1985, he was elected to the prestigious Black Belt Hall of Fame for teaching the legendary Japanese ninja martial arts. In 2015 he was the sole recipient of the Martial Arts Industry Association (MAIA) Lifetime Achievement Award.

Hayes is the author of 20 books which translate the timeless knowledge of the East into pragmatic lessons for contemporary Western life. He regularly served in the 1990s as personal protection escort and security advisor for the Dalai Lama of Tibet.

The author and the Dalai Lama.

He is married to Rumiko Urata, who graduated from Sophia University in Tokyo, Japan. She often joins him in the dojo and on the road, sharing the legacy of the ninja martial arts tradition. They have two daughters and five grandchildren.

Bojutsu long staff method in the author's private house dojo.

Hayes spends much of the year traveling the world as a teacher, translating his background in martial and meditation arts into practical lessons for handling the pressures and uncertainties of life.

StephenKHayes.com

Published by Tuttle Publishing, an imprint of Periplus Editions (HK) Ltd.

www.tuttlepublishing.com

Photographs by P.R. Frank

Library of Congress Cataloging in Process

ISBN 978-4-8053-1537-8
Distributed by

North America
Tuttle Publishing
364 Innovation Drive, North Clarendon, VT 05759-9436 U.S.A.
Tel: 1 (802) 773-8930; Fax: 1 (802) 773-6993 info@tuttlepublishing.com;
www.tuttlepublishing.com

Japan
Tuttle Publishing
Yaekari Building, 3F, 5-4-12 Osaki, Shinagawa-ku, Tokyo 141-0032
Tel: (81) 3 5437-0171; Fax: (81) 3 5437-0755 sales@tuttle.co.jp; www.tuttle.co.jp

Asia Pacific
Berkeley Books Pte Ltd, 3 Kallang Sector #04-01, Singapore 349278
Tel: (65) 6741-2178; Fax: (65) 6741-2179 inquiries@periplus.com.sg;
www.periplus.com

First edition
23 22 21 20 5 4 3 2 1
Printed in Malaysia 1910VP

THE TUTTLE STORY
"Books to Span the East and West"

Our core mission at Tuttle Publishing is to create books which bring people together one page at a time. Tuttle was founded in 1832 in the small New England town of Rutland, Vermont (USA). Our fundamental values remain as strong today as they were then—to publish best-in-class books informing the English-speaking world about the countries and peoples of Asia. The world has become a smaller place today and Asia's economic, cultural and political influence has expanded, yet the need for meaningful dialogue and information about this diverse region has never been greater. Since 1948, Tuttle has been a leader in publishing books on the cultures, arts, cuisines, languages and literatures of Asia. Our authors and photographers have won numerous awards and Tuttle has published thousands of books on subjects ranging from martial arts to paper crafts. We welcome you to explore the wealth of information available on Asia at **www.tuttlepublishing.com**.